Georges Bernage

THE D.DAY LANDING BEACHES

The guide

Translation: John Lee

HEIMDAL

— Conceived and written by : Georges Bernage

— Translation: John Lee

— Production : Jean-Luc Leleu

— Maps : Bernard Paich

— Layout : Francine Gautier and Erik Groult

— Composition : Christel Lebret

— Photoengraving : Christian Caira,
                   Philippe Gazagne and Christel Lebret

— Graphics : Philippe Gazagne

— Illustrations : Bundesarchiv, Koblenz (BA.)
                Imperial War Museum (IWM.)
                National Archives, Washington (NA.)
                Public Archives of Canada, Ottawa (PAC.)
                Collection Heimdal

Editions Heimdal - Château de Damigny - BP 61350 - 14406 BAYEUX Cedex
Tel. : +33 (0)231 516 868 - Fax : +33 (0)231 516 860 - E mail : Editions.Heimdal@wanadoo.fr

ISBN 2 84048 137-5

US Navy

Contents

Normandy under occupation

1. Bayeux, the now Hôtel du Luxembourg at the time was Soldatenheim Bayeux, the German's soldier's center. (E. Groult coll.).

2. Field-Marshal Erwin Rommel, commander of Heeresgruppe B which confronted the Allied landing in Normandy. (Heimdal coll.).

3. In the spring of 1944, in Normandy, the occupying forces were no more than a pale shadow of the all-conquering armored divisions of May 1940. Here we see the artillerymen of 716. Infanterie-Division with their horses. (Heimdal coll.)

May 10, 1940; the Wehrmacht launched its attack on the West, entering the Netherlands, Belgium and Luxembourg. The French army would be defeated within a matter of weeks. And, on June 7, 1940, General Rommel and his 7.Panzer-Division entered Normandy; in an astonishing quirk of fate, four years later to the day, here was Rommel himself in command of Heeresgruppe B facing the Allied landing in Normandy! On June 11, 1940, Rommel received the surrender of 51st Highland Division at Saint-Valéry-en-Caux; this division, having been reconstituted, took part in the Battle of Normandy in June 1944. On June 19, 1940, Rommel received the surrender of French troops at Cherbourg; General von Schlieben surrendered at Cherbourg on June 26, 1944.

Following the signing of the armistice between France and Germany, Normandy was densely occupied by German troops, who set up Kriegsmarine bases there and later coastal artillery batteries, and later still, strongpoints all along the coast. Several divisions were stationed there. The presence of so many occupying troops in the coastal sector was an incitement to a number of young Normans to join the Resistance.

Very early on, in 1940, the British intelligence services were in need of information regarding the status and numbers of German troops. At the time, they feared a German invasion of England (Operation "Seelöwe"). Then came the attempted landing at Dieppe in 1942 and finally the planned landing in Nor-

mandy ("Overlord"). So the Allies set up a structured network of information services across Normandy, the heaviest concentration of its kind in France. Thus, from the summer of 1942 to the spring of 1944, Normandy totaled 74 branches of French and Allied networks under the BCRA, the SOE, MI6 or the OSS. Intelligence of crucial importance for the success of the landing was dispatched to England - lists of German defenses, a map of the Atlantic Wall from Cherbourg to Honfleur, the location of V1 launch pads, etc... From January 1943 to May 1944, Allied intelligence received nearly 300 reports with information that made an invaluable contribution towards the success of Operation Overlord.

And, despite the density of the occupying forces, the resistance had over 200 groups in Normandy, all helping the Allied forces. Over the five départements, their numbers totaled 16,504 men, only 5,860 of whom were properly armed, but with no heavy equipment. The wooded, inland Orne département, had 3,750 underground fighters, around a thousand of whom were properly armed. The Manche département, on the other hand, with its long coastline, only had 1,441 volunteers. On June 1, 1944, the Normandy resistance "Action" groups were organized into 14 maquis and 96 irregular forces and groups. Five plans were devised in London to assist the Allied landings:

- Green Plan: Sabotage of the railways. They were sabotaged in 31 places on priority lines.

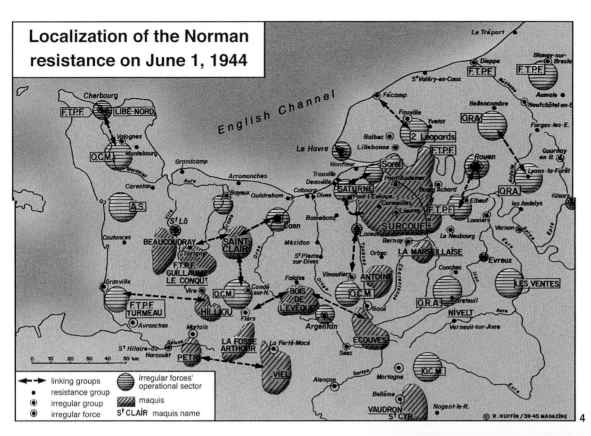

Localization of the Norman resistance on June 1, 1944

4. The Resistance networks were unevenly spread across Normandy. They found it harder to establish themselves in the coastal sectors. (Heimdal and R. Ruffin).

- Blue Plan: Interruption of energy distribution. 9 transformers and 52 pylons were destroyed, depriving many defensive coastal positions of electricity.

- Purple Plan: Cutting of overhead and underground telephone links. 94 interventions left the telephone system in chaos. At Saint-Lô, the commander of 84 (r.) Armee-Korps, General Marcks, was unable to get in touch with his regimental CPs and coastal strongpoints.

- Bibendum (or Tortoise) Plan: To block or paralyze units coming up to the front in reinforcement. Barrages and handfuls of special nails were used to hold up the convoys.

- Red Plan: Launch of guerrilla action. Volunteers from the Surcouf maquis came up among others against Major Steinbach's battalion stationed at Le Pin.

General Eisenhower reported to the effect that the help of the Norman resistance in the preparation and landing operations, their contribution to the battle to establish a firm beachhead, their support during the great offensives against Caen and Avranches, their assistance in crossing the Seine, weighed decisively in the collapse of the German front.

BCRA: Bureau Central de Renseignement et d'Action, the Free French Secret Service's Central Bureau of Information and Action.

SOE: Special Operations Executive, British organization set up to train resistance groups in enemy-occupied countries.

MI6: British Secret Intelligence Service.

OSS: Office of Strategic Services, MI6's American counterpart.

5. A maquis radio operator listens to personal messages as he awaits the message announcing the landing. (Heimdal)

Atlantic Wall

1. Contemporary works of propaganda. The Germans exaggerated the strength of the so-called "Wall" to intimidate the Allies. (BP coll.).

2. The position at Etretat (Et 05) is typical of the German design of beach defenses: a 75 Pak 40 enfilades a beach bristling with obstacles. (BA).

3. The range-finding post of the Longues-sur-Mer battery (4./HKAA 1260) overlooking the sea with its stocky outline set into the cliff top. It was used as a setting for the film "The Longest Day". (EG/Heimdal).

German propaganda had vastly exaggerated the reality of the "Atlantic Wall" (Atlantikwall), which also became known as "Fortress Europe" or "The Steel Coast" (Die Stählerne Küste, a contemporary book title). As we know, except the Douvres-la-Délivrande radar station which was a thorn in the Allies' flank for a week, this "wall" held out for only a few hours on June 6, 1944; but despite its weaknesses and gaps in many sectors, the Allies did not underestimate the problem. It caused the landing to be postponed, particularly after the tragic failure at Dieppe in 1942. The British, spearheaded by 79th Armored Division, went on to devise special vehicles to tackle it, and extremely useful they proved. The Allies decided to land where the wall was at its weakest, in Normandy and not in the Straits of Dover where the distance from England to the continent was the shortest.

As early as 1942 the Orne estuary and Cherbourg were earmarked by the Germans as sectors needing fortification. In Upper Normandy, Le Havre

and Dieppe harbors had been under the control of the Kriegsmarine since the occupation started. Although Sealion (Seelöwe), the plan for the invasion of England, had been abandoned by the end of 1940, these ports remained important bases for the sea war against the British Empire. After the attempted landing of Anglo-Canadian forces at Dieppe on August 19, 1942, the German command had heavily reinforced these bases, as obviously the Allies would need these ports for their supplies in the event of a landing. Thus major ports like Cherbourg and Le Havre in Normandy were turned into fortresses (Festungen). Cherbourg was defended by powerful coastal artillery and would be quite capable of withstanding an assault from the sea. On the other hand, the land defenses were very poor, and as it turned out, Cherbourg was captured from that quarter within a few days at the end of June 1944.

From 1943 onwards, with German reversals in the East and Allied landings in North Africa and later on in Italy (Sicily on July 10, 1943; Salerno on September 9, 1943), it became obvious the invasion would in fact take place on the beaches, which therefore had to be fortified as well. First, at more or less regular intervals, artillery batteries were set in concrete pits, but these became more vulnerable to air attack as the Allied Air Forces became more and more efficient. Gradually, concrete casemates sheltered the guns, which had the effect of reducing their range to the casemates' embrasure width.

Command of these batteries was not uniform. Owing to its experience of coastal artillery, the Kriegsmarine was put in charge of setting up a number of batteries, mostly the larger ones. Some few strongpoints even had rotating steel casemates equipped with very large naval guns, e.g. Le Havre (Biéville) or Guernsey (Mirus). Others, generally static batteries, were entrusted to the land army (Heer) to be operated by the divisions defending the coast. The concrete casemates were built to

the Heer's own plans, which explains the huge diversity of casemate types to be found dotted across Normandy. Also, the Atlantic Wall extended over a considerable distance, from the North Cape in Norway to the Franco-Spanish border. The enormous requirement for guns to equip the batteries pushed the Germans to take everything they could find, mostly captured guns, French 155mm guns, Russian 122mm guns and numerous other models, the best of which were Kriegsmarine naval guns from decommissioned ships. All the different kinds of shells to be supplied caused endless problems.

On the coastal strip, the beach sectors were equipped with lighter but denser defenses. Rocky coasts and those protected by high bluffs hardly needed further defense, and so received little fortification. In those sectors favorable for a landing, resistance nests (Wn, short for Widerstandsnest) and strongpoints (Stp, short for Stützpunk) were established. The strongest defenses were provided by guns, the size of which varied from 50mm up to 75mm and even in some cases the 88mm gun. Most of the guns were sited under concrete casemates, the embrasure of which had the peculiarity of not facing the sea, so as to prevent a direct hit from Allied naval artillery. The embrasures were arranged so the guns fired along the beach and often two strongpoints provided crossfire. Between the casemates - which proved especially troublesome for the Allied forces and had to be reduced with the help of amphibious and special tanks - lay the beach defenses. On the seafront was a concrete anti-tank wall to slow down or stop progression of tanks and even men coming off the beaches. Minefields and barbed wire were also placed for the same purpose. Behind this concrete wall were to be found various infantry positions, chiefly Ringstände, circular positions called "Tobruks" by the Allies. They were concrete shelters with a circular opening on top, in which an infantryman could position himself with a machine-gun. Some types of "Tobruk" were more spacious and could accommodate mortars or even anti-aircraft guns. Many concrete buildings were built as command posts, observation posts, personnel shelters, shelters for searchlights, garages, first aid stations and ammunition stores. These various shelters were linked by trenches behind networks of barbed wire, minefields and automatic flame throwers.

Casemates and shelters were often camouflaged, with trompe-l'œil painting, imitation stone, turf and structures to make a casemate look like a harmless house. But all this building work, from "Tobruks" to big artillery casemates, needed a colossal effort. The Todt Organization, the Third Reich's giant public works concern, was in charge of the job. It was structured by region so as to monitor the building works. By the end of 1942, OBL Cherbourg employed in Normandy 9,902 persons including 972 Germans and 7,722 Frenchmen. But, despite these forces, out of 1,375 planned major works, only 10%

4. Remnants of "imitation stone" camouflage paint on one of the Azeville battery casemates.

5. Two "Tobruks" (circular machine-gun emplacements) on the beach at Riva-Bella.

6. German stake used to fence off a field at Longues-sur-Mer.

7. Asnelles-sur-Mer (Gold Beach). This casemate for a 50mm gun has a thick concrete wall facing seaward. The embrasures were placed so as to rake the beaches. (Photos EG/Heimdal).

Background photo: sketch by Rommel showing how glider obstacles were to be arranged. (BA).

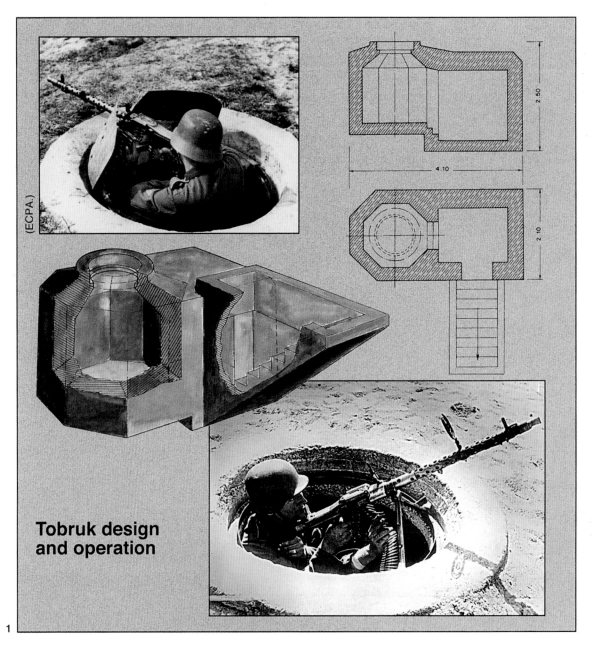

Tobruk design and operation

1. The Ringstand (circular position, which the Allies called the "Tobruk") was the simplest of the German defenses. A machine-gun was placed inside the round opening as a ground or anti-aircraft defense. Most of the concrete shelters had a Ringstand for close defense. (Heimdal).

2. Example of absorptive form. To speed up casemate building work, the Germans devised an "absorptive form "in breeze blocks. Instead of shuttering with planks, the metal reinforcement was place between two breeze block walls and filled with concrete. Here at Ver-sur-Mer, the Mont Fleury battery (Wn 35 a) was left unfinished, showing the breeze block walls awaiting the concrete.

---

were finished by then. In February 1944, OBL Cherbourg employed 19,619 men (15,081 of them were foreign workers). When the landings came, only 2/3 of the program had been completed and many building works remained unfinished, at Pointe du Hoc, Saint Marcouf, Fermanville etc. At the Mont-Fleury battery at Ver-sur-Mer, some casemates were no more than breeze block walls, built as "absorptive form" within which concrete was to be poured. In fact, the Atlantic Wall was not a continuous line but a string of nests of resistance interspersed with weak points.

Beach obstacles

In front of these fortifications, Field-Marshal Rommel had obstacles set up on the beaches. He been appointed inspector of fortifications for both the Atlantic Wall and the Südwall (the latter on the Mediterranean coast) late in 1943, and stated "the front line is on the beach". As early as January 15, 1944 he was himself sketching various types of obstacles he wished to see installed on the beaches. From January 16 to 19, 1944, he conducted a tour of inspection in Normandy from Mont Canisy to Le Tréport. He revisited Normandy from May 9 to 11, when he visited Houlgate, Ouistreham, Colleville, Longues-sur-Mer, Saint-Laurent (future Omaha Beach), Pointe du Hoc, Azeville, Saint-Marcouf, Quinéville, Morsalines, La Pernelle and Cherbourg - but all too late. The Allies landed three weeks later. He did however, feverishly hurry erection of these beach obstacles.

3. The beach at Varreville (Utah Beach) still covered with stakes in June 1944. The one in the foreground has a mine on top of it. (GB/Heimdal).

4. A concrete tetrahedron spiked with sheet steel to rip out the bottom of the landing craft. (EG/Heimdal).

5. Field-Marshal Rommel in the Cotentin Peninsula during a tour of inspection on May 10 and 11, 1944. On the left, the bespectacled General Marcks, commander of the German 84th Corps. (Heimdal coll.).

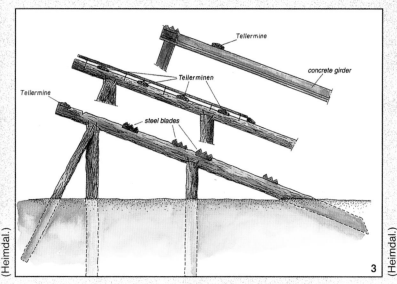

Tellermine
Tellerminen
concrete girder
Tellermine
steel blades

(Heimdal.)

3

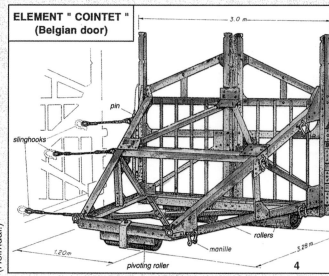

3.0 m
pin
slinghooks
rollers
1.20 m
manille
3.28 m.
pivoting roller

(Heimdal.)

4

(BA.)

3

7

11

Mined stakes

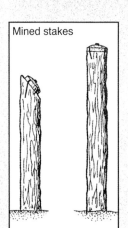

Offshore were magnetic mines (1) fastened by chains, then antisubmarine nets (2). On the beach itself, 25ft long tree trunks (3) were driven into the beach pointing seawards (in Steven Spielberg's film Saving Private Ryan they were back to front!) and provided with steel saw-teeth or mines to blow up landing craft. This they did to particularly deadly effect in the Juno sector. There were also just stakes leaning slightly and with a mine on top. Other obstacles included: Element Cointet (a gate acting as a barrage, hence the nickname "Belgian gate" (4); an obstacle with a rail on top containing a mine exploded by pressure on the rail (5); concrete or steel tetrahedra (6); Czech hedgehogs (7); ram logs (8); concrete pyramids (9); Curtoir rails (15); metal friezes (10); and concrete tetrapods (11). To the rear, in the diagram, can be seen the concrete antitank wall (12), mines (13), barbed wire (14) and flame throwers (16). These obstacles were only partly set in position but often fulfilled their role against the landing craft. (Heimdal).

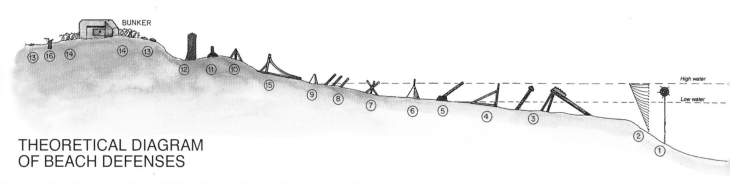

THEORETICAL DIAGRAM
OF BEACH DEFENSES

The troops behind the "Wall"

Static infantry divisions had been placed behind the Atlantic Wall to ensure its defense. But reinforcement needs for the eastern front regularly led to levy out the western forces. So, by spring of 1944, the infantry divisions behind the "Wall" were very poor, i.e. old or inadequately trained soldiers, forces that should have been withdrawn from duty etc. For example, in the Cherbourg area, there was a battalion of "belly-achers". Often, due to these levies, regiments were not up to strength and could only muster two battalions instead of three. Also, battalions of volunteers were recruited in the USSR to fill the gaps. Nine of these battalions were stationed between Dieppe and the Cherbourg peninsula and a Russian brigade stationed south of Coutances. The 835th North Caucasian Battalion was NE of Le Havre, the 441st Russian Battalion between Asnelles and Courseulles (future Juno and Gold Beaches), and the 795th Georgian Battalion around Turqueville (future Utah Beach). Another Georgian battalion, the 747th, was north of Coutances. About one third of the front line troops were volunteers from the USSR, and Allied soldiers upon coming ashore often had the surprise of fighting a Russian or a Georgian soldier rather than a German soldier. These volunteers had various motives. Some joined to fight Soviet power, either as anticommunists in the case of the Russians, or out of a desire for independence in the case of the Georgians and Chechens (already!) of the North Caucasian Battalion, or quite simply to escape the rigors of captivity.

In the spring of 1944, Lower Normandy was controlled by German 84th Corps whose commander, General der Artillerie Erich Marcks, had his headquarters in Saint Lô. At the time however, he only had four infantry divisions at his disposal.

- 716. Infanterie-Division was stationed on the coast of Calvados between the Orne the Vire estuaries. This division was recruited in the Rhineland and Westphalia. It was under the command of Generalleutenant Wilhelm Richter (command post in the quarries where the Caen Memorial now stands). It comprised only two infantry regiments, IR 726 and IR 736, and it had a strength of only 10,000 men (half of an Allied division), with support from two battalions of Osttruppen (USSR volunteers), the 441st and 642nd Battalions.

- 709. Infanterie Division was stationed on the eastern coast of the Cherbourg peninsula between Cherbourg and Carentan facing what was to be Utah Beach. It was recruited in Hesse and under the command of Generalleutnant Karl-Wilhelm von Schlieben. This division was less undermanned than the one above, having received a third infantry regiment, Infanterie Regiment 919, late in 1943. Its two other infantry regiments were IR 729 and IR 739, but at 36, the average age of its soldiers was rather high. It also had two Georgian Ost battalions, to complete its strength.

- 243. Infanterie Division, on the west coast of Cherbourg peninsula, was formed in Austria and had three infantry regiments (IR 920, IR 921 and IR 922) placed under the command of Generalleutnant Heinz Hellmich.

- Lastly, 319. Infanterie Division, under Generlleutnant Rudolph von Schmettow, had extra strength but it was stationed in the Channel Islands and did not play any role in the Battle of Normandy. It was still there when the Germans surrendered in 1945.

So this sector of Normandy was defended by only three poor quality divisions. The German High Command thought the landing would take place in the Pas de Calais where the distance to England is very short. The eight German divisions there had strength in depth. Lower Normandy was obviously the "poor relation "but, not knowing the Allies' intentions, the Germans had to hedge their bets. Still, as the archives later revealed, Rommel and Hitler had a hunch that it could all yet happen on the Normandy beaches, and a few weeks before the landings the following three infantry units were sent to reinforce the sector.

- 352. Infanterie Division, formed in November 1943, was sent to the Calvados coast between Bayeux and Carentan. It reinforced to the west the weak 716. Infanterie Division. This new unit, under Generalleutnant Dietrich Kraiss (CP at Le Molay Littry), had three infantry regiments (IR 914, IR 915 and IR 916). The presence of this division surprised the Allied troops, who had to fight it on Omaha Beach, thereby putting the American landing in jeopardy in this sector.

- 91. Luftlande-Division was an airborne division formed at the beginning of 1944. Led by Generalleutnant Wilhelm Falley, it had only two infantry regiments (IR 1057 and IR 1058). This division was initially intended to be airborne but was in fact infantry trained to fight against paratroopers. In May 1944, it was located in the middle of the Cherbourg peninsula, between 709 ID and 243 ID. Another nasty surprise for the Allies, as the division indeed confronted the American paratroopers.

- Lastly, Fallschirmjäger-Regiment 6, a paratroop regiment commanded by Major Friedrich von der Heydte, had left Brittany and was stationed in the Carentan area. It was one of the first German units to see action on D-Day against the American paras.

Alongside this corps attached to 7th Army, a few other units attached to German 81st Corps (General der Panzertruppen Adolf Kuntzen, CP at Canteleu near Rouen) fought on the eastern flank of the Allied sector, in particular 711. Infanterie Division, under Generalleutnant Josef Reichert, and two infantry regiments (IR 731 and IR 781). It also had an Ost battalion, the 781st, formed from Asian volunteers from Turkmenistan. This battalion was attached to IR 731.The division was stationed between Cabourg and Honfleur and faced the paras of the British 6th Airborne Division.

The Panzers

Besides these coastal defense divisions, the German headquarters had two armored divisions in reserve in this sector.

- 21. Panzer-Division, led by Generalleutnant Edgar Feuchtinger (CP at Saint Pierre-sur-Dives) was in place near the beaches, between Caen and Falaise. It comprised a tank regiment, Panzer-Regiment 100 (its code number had been changed to PR 22) whose strength was not complete. It only had about a hundred Panzer IVs and 23 obsolete French S-35 tanks. Near the British landing beaches (Sword Beach)

General der Artillerie Erich Marcks, (CP at Saint Lô), commander of 84 (r.) Armee-Korps.

Generalleutenant Wilhelm Richter (CP at Caen), commander of 716. Infanterie-Division.

Generalleutenant Dietrich Kraiss (CP at Le Molay-Littry), commander of 352. Infanterie-Division, newly arrived in the sector.

this panzer division was a reserve of Army Group B (General-Feldmarschall Gerd von Rundstedt, CP at Saint Germain-en-Laye). It was alerted at 00.35 on June 6 but its tank regiment took sixteen hours to launch a counterattack!

- 12. SS Panzer-Division (led by SS-Brigadeführer Fritz Witt) had a powerful tank regiment but this elite division was in reserve with OKW (the German Armed Forces High Command). It set off only after a long delay and leading elements of this division did not reach Caen until the evening of D-Day. This division was stationed in the Eure département.

Finally, two battalions of independent tanks were based in the Cherbourg peninsula but being equipped with old French tanks they did not play any role. As for the Panzer-Lehr-Division, based in the Eure-et-Loir département, it saw no action on D-Day.

Above: This Panzer IV was used to instruct tank crews of SS-Panzer-Regiment 12. at the Mailly camp in June 1943. (Heimdal coll.).

Below: Spring 1944, at Saint-Martin-de-Fresnay, midway between Lisieux and Saint-Pierre-sur-Dives, a Panzer IV of Panzer-Regiment 100 (21. Panzer-Division) has stopped outside a cafe and grocery store to fill up with... camembert cheeses! As the Germans said, they lived like gods in France. The tank is an obsolete Panzer IV Ausf. C with a short-barreled gun, like the ones that fought in France in 1940. This panzer division had a number of old tanks. (BA).

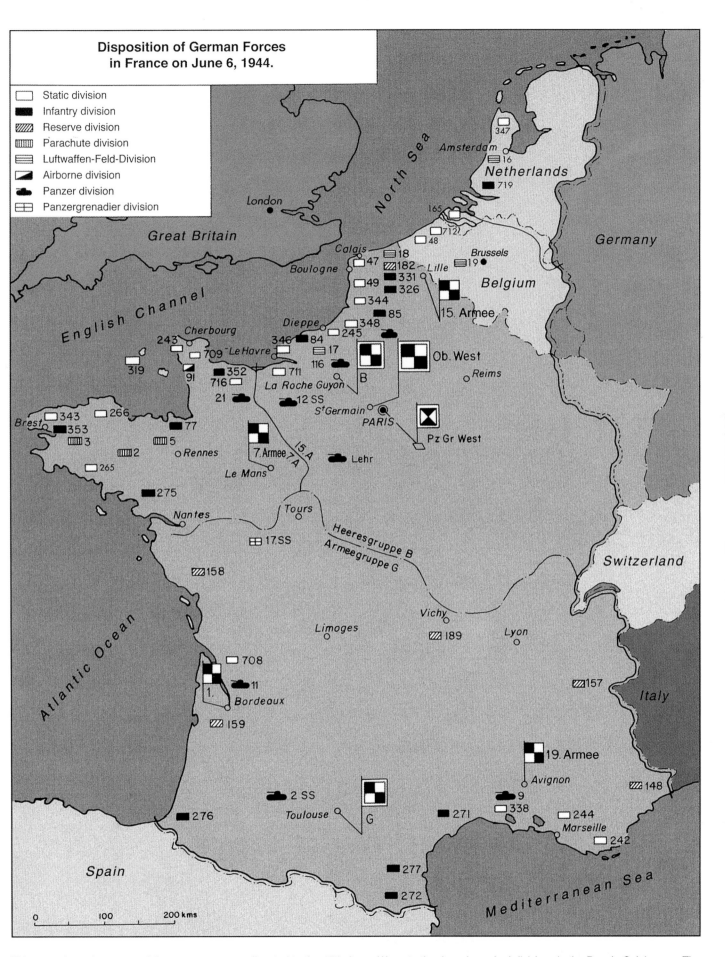

Disposition of German Forces in France on June 6, 1944.

Static division
Infantry division
Reserve division
Parachute division
Luftwaffen-Feld-Division
Airborne division
Panzer division
Panzergrenadier division

This map shows how most of the resources were allocated to the 15th Army. We note the densely packed divisions in the Pas de Calais area. The 7th Army, in charge of the sector where the Allies were to land, is not so strong. However, Hitler feared a landing in Normandy, even though the high command was focusing on the Pas de Calais, and sent in two new divisions to reinforce the defenses in western Normandy: 91. Luftlande-Division and 352. Infanterie-Division. (Heimdal map).

Overlord

1. The Allied chiefs-of-staff at Bushey Park on February 12, 1944. Left to right: Generals Omar N. Bradley, Tedder, Eisenhower, Montgomery, Air Chief Marshal Sir Trafford Leigh-Mallory and Major-General W. Bedell-Smith. (US Army).

2. After several weeks of hesitation, Roosevelt's mind was made up and he appointed Eisenhower, then commander-in-chief in the Mediterranean, to take overall command of Operation Overlord, at Supreme Headquarters, Allied Expeditionary Forces (SHAEF). (IWM).

Back in July 1940, Winston Churchill had set up Combined Operations headquarters. On August 19, 1942, the attempted landing at Dieppe ended in bloody failure, although teaching a lot of hard lessons meantime. November of that same year saw the landing in north Africa, later followed by Sicily and Italy. Churchill wanted to carry on in this direction as far as the Balkans. But at the Tehran Conference in December 1943, the Russians insisted on a landing in France, as Stalin feared that the Allies would establish themselves in the Balkans and central Europe, which he wanted to keep for himself.

Accordingly, two landing operations were planned in France: in Normandy (Overlord) and Provence (Anvil). The two operations were at first scheduled to coincide but owing to a shortage of landing ships, Overlord was given priority and finally Anvil was not launched until after Overlord.

So the planned Normandy landing was made the number one priority. General Eisenhower, the Allied Supreme Commander at SHAEF, was based in London. General Bernard Montgomery was placed in command of the ground forces and 21st Army Group. General Omar Bradley was to command the American ground forces of First US Army, and Lieutenant-General Miles C. Dempsey the British ground forces of Second British Army. Admiral Bertram H. Ramsay would command the Allied naval forces and Air Chief Marshal Trafford Leigh-Mallory the Allied air forces. The initial plan for the operation was presented by Eisenhower on February 1, 1944. The plans for the operation were complete by mid-March.

At the Trident conference in Washington in May 1943, the landing sector was chosen for Overlord: Normandy was preferred to the Pas de Calais. The German divisions were much more densely packed in the latter sector, and most of all, there were not enough beaches and ports to enable a rapid build-up of the lodgment area. It was accordingly decided to land between the Orne and Vire estuaries, with a first wave of five divisions, two airborne and three seaborne (one American and two British). Twenty follow-up divisions were to be at the ready in the UK. Extra resources were made available. Late in January 1944, Eisenhower reported on the resources that would ultimately be committed:

three airborne and five seaborne divisions (two American and three British). The landing sector was extended from 40 km (25 mi) to 60 km (37 mi), from the Orne estuary to the east coast of the Cotentin peninsula. The airborne divisions were to seal off the landing sector, protecting it on either flank during the night before the amphibious operation. Thus, from east to west:

Second British Army was to land between Caen and Bayeux on the left flank; this would be I British Corps with 6th Airborne Division on the east bank of the Orne, 3rd British Division and 27th Armored Brigade in the leading wave, followed by the commandos of 1st Special Service Brigade, 51st (Highland) Division and 4th Armored Brigade on **Sword Beach.** The 3rd Canadian Division and 2nd Canadian Armored Brigade were to come ashore at **Juno Beach** in the leading wave, followed by the commandos of 4th Special Service Brigade. On the right wing, XXX British Corps was to land at **Gold Beach** with 50th (Northumbrian) Division and 8th Armored Brigade in the leading wave, followed by 7th Armored Division and 49th (West Riding) Division.

First US Army was to land between Bayeux and the east of the Cotentin peninsula. On the left flank, V Corps would land at **Omaha Beach** with 1st Infantry Division and elements of 29th Infantry Division in the leading wave, followed by the rest of 29th Division and 2nd Infantry Division and two Ranger battalions, on that beach and at Pointe du Hoc. On the right flank, VII Corps would land at **Utah Beach** with 4th Infantry Division in the leading wave, followed by 9th Infantry Division, 90th Infantry Division and 79th Infantry Division. Two airborne divisions, 82nd and 101st Airborne, were to set up a bridgehead in that sector.

The choice of Normandy for Operation Overlord also helped to deceive the Germans. Operation Fortitude, launched by the Allies, led them to believe the landing was coming in the Pas de Calais area, thus pinning down German divisions in that sector.

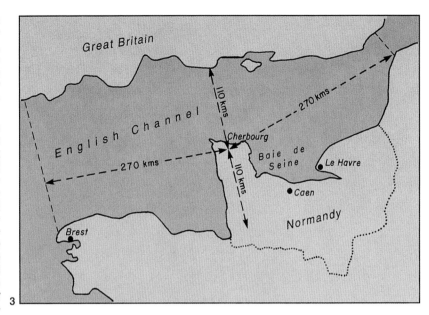

3

4

5

3. The Bay of the Seine offered four main advantages: - the port of Cherbourg with its large roadstead; - a whole series of broad beaches with exits lining up between Saint-Vaast-la-Hougue and Ouistreham, the eastern side of the Cotentin peninsula being protected from the prevailing westerly winds; - within striking distance of the coast of southern England; - a hinterland suitable for establishing airfields. On the down side, the thick hedgerows were to prove a severe handicap. (Heimdal).

4. An LCA; 485 of this type of landing craft were available for Overlord. (US Navy).

5. Exercise on a beach in southern England; on the right, a Sherman DD tank. (US Navy).

Hobart's "Funnies"

Emblem of 79th Armored Division, a bull's head, painted on the vehicles.

Sir Percy Hobart (1885-1957).

After the failed raid on Dieppe, the British commanders were forced to give some thought to how a successful landing might be achieved. Thus, in April 1943, the 79th Armored Division under Major-General Sir Percy C.S. Hobart, was selected to research specialized vehicles designed to facilitate landing operations: tanks for the engineers, amphibious tanks, tanks to clear minefields... These were the "Funnies", a name disliked by "Hobo", as the general himself was nicknamed.

Following tests on the eve of D-Day, 79th Armored Division was equipped with various specialized tanks. They were capable of carrying out the following tasks, particularly the A.V.R.E.s (Armored Vehicle Royal Engineers) - converted Churchill tanks:

- Walls and other obstacles were smashed with "flying dustbins" fired by the A.V.R.E. "Petard", a Churchill tank on which the gun was replaced with a 290 mm mortar which knocked out guns, concrete obstacles and any defensive positions.

- The S.B.G. assault bridge was a Churchill tank chassis on which was mounted a Small Box Girder (S.B.G.) bridge that could be unfolded to pass over obstacles like antitank ditches.

- One Churchill A.V.R.E. could also carry faggots for dropping into a ditch which could then be crossed more easily.

- Another Churchill A.V.R.E., called the "Bobbin" or "Carpet-layer", unrolled a canvas roadway to avoid landing vehicles getting bogged down.

- There were also minefields to be cleared for crossing; for this there were two designs, the "Bullshorn Plough", a Sherman tank fitted with a kind of plough on the front to sweep up any mines on the beach, and the "Flail", or "Crab". This more effective design involved a Sherman fitted with a rotary drum on the front with whirling chains to explode any mines.

– There was also the "Crocodile", a Churchill flamethrower tank.

– Last but not least, and probably the most surprising of all, the Sherman DD ("Duplex Drive") amphibious tank was fitted with a canvas skirt and a propeller enabling it to swim. Although many were lost in heavy seas on D-Day, this was the weapon that most surprised the Germans, tanks coming up from the sea like boats...

---

1. On December 9, 1943, during an exercise, a Churchill A.V.R.E. carrying a bundle of faggots. (IWM).

2. This Churchill A.V.R.E. has placed faggots on the far side of a concrete antitank wall to soften its landing on the other side. (IWM).

3. A Churchill Carpet-Layer tank during training on April 26, 1944; the carpet was designed for crossing soft sand. (IWM).

4. A 290mm mortar mounted on a Churchill A.V.R.E. with, on the right, a "Petard "to blast beach obstacles or concrete works. (IWM).

79th Armored Division

The division had three specialized armored brigades made available as and where needed to the larger units.

- 30th Armored Brigade had four regiments equipped with Crabs (flail tanks): 22nd Dragoons, 1st Lothian and Border Horse Yeomanry, 2nd C.L.Y. (Westminster Dragoons), 141st R.A.C. (The Buffs).

- 1st Tank Brigade, with 11th R.T.R., 42nd R.T.R. and 49th R.T.R., had C.D.L. tanks (carrying a searchlight).

- 1st Assault Brigade R.E. had Churchill A.V.R.E. tanks allocated to 54th Assault Regt. R.E., 6th Assault Regt. R.E., and 42nd Assault Regt. R.E.

The DD tanks were issued to various units.

All these special vehicles played a substantial role in the D-Day landings. Apart from the DD tanks used by the Americans, they were only used by the British, who put down their successful landing in their sector partly to these vehicles.

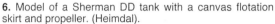

6. Model of a Sherman DD tank with a canvas flotation skirt and propeller. (Heimdal).

7. A DD tank preserved at Courseulles. (IWM).

5. A Sherman Crab tank during training in England before D-Day. The long "flails" plough up the soil to explode any mines. (IWM).

8. A Churchill Crocodile tank during training in England on April 20, 1944: the flammable liquid in the trailer had a range of 120 yards and burned its target for around ten minutes. (Heimdal).

9. A Churchill A.V.R.E. at Graye-sur-Mer (Juno Beach) not far from the Lorraine Cross. (Heimdal).

The Allies used all kinds of landing equipment in Normandy. Here we see some of the 2,583 DUKW amphibious trucks that plied continuously between the ships and the shore, bringing in a constant flow of matériel. (US Navy).

Naval forces involved in Overlord

The landing ships were so important to the success of Overlord that the date of the operation was deferred several times to leave time to build enough ships. A varied range of special landing craft were designed. Altogether, 4,308 landing vessels were mobilized for this operation, representing 15% of all Allied shipping.

They included over 1,700 light landing craft:

- 486 LCAs (Landing Craft, Assault): about 40 feet long, it could be beached directly carrying 35 men and half a ton of equipment.

- 839 LCVPs (Landing Craft, Vehicle Personnel): about 40 feet long, it could carry either 36 men or a lorry, or five tons of equipment.

- 45 LCA (HR)s: a version designed to explode German mines and booby-traps.

- 145 LCP (L)s: used to set smoke screens to camouflage the landing fleet.

Large LSI, APA and AKA type ships, transport along their flanks the assault craft that will take both soldiers and equipment to the beaches. Here we see LCVPs being lowered from the side of this ship. (US Navy).

- 76 LCSs: an LCA version lending supporting fire, armed with either a smoke mortar and two machine-guns (LCS-M), or a tank turret and antitank weaponry (LCS-L), or two 20mm guns and an antitank gun (LCS-L2).

- 486 LCMs (Landing Craft, Mechanized): these were slightly bigger landing craft, around 43 feet long, carrying either a 30-ton tank or a truck.

Other landing craft were bigger still:

- 873 LCTs (Landing Craft, Tank): about 200 feet long, it could carry three or four tanks, or trucks.

- 265 LCIs (Landing Craft, Infantry): there were two models, the LCI(L) (large) measuring around 165 feet in length and carrying nearly 200 men and 32 tons of equipment, and the LCI(S) (small) measuring around 100 feet in length and carrying nearly 100 men.

There were also several dozen LCT and LCI versions lending supporting fire.

- 236 LSTs (Landing Ship, Tank): fitted with cranes, a gate and a ramp in the bows used to land tanks and other vehicles directly, it was about 300 feet long and could transport 1750 tons of cargo in the hold and 350 tons on deck with a maximum load of 500 tons when landing directly onto the beach.

- There were also LSIs (Landing Ship, Infantry) which brought troops and LCAs and LCMs up to the coast. The APA (Auxiliary Personnel, Attack) was the American equivalent of the LSI, and could carry about fifteen LCVPs. The AKA (Auxiliary Ship Cargo, Attack) was an LSI specializing in the transport of equipment.

In addition to all these landing craft and landing ships, there were 470 LVTs and 2,583 amphibious DUKW trucks.

These 4,308 landing vessels were to play a crucial role in the success of the operation, as they were able to bring ashore all at once not only men, but also a large number of wheeled and tracked vehicles.

The fleet in support of the landing

There was also a mighty navy in support of the landing operations. It included 238 large warships, 221 smaller vessels, 200 minesweepers and 805 merchant navy ships on top of the 4,308 landing craft and ships, making a grand total of over 5,700 vessels of every size. The vast majority of the warships (almost 80%) belonged to the Royal Navy, the rest came from the US Navy (16.5%), France, Holland, Norway and Poland.

Organizing all these fleets raised some complex problems. An extra 130 landing stages had to be built in England. 48 hours before D-Day, the minesweepers had to clear 400 to 1200 meter-wide channels and the fleet to split according to beach sectors: Force S for Sword, J for Juno, G for Gold and L for the follow-up division heading for the Eastern (British) zone with 3 battleships, one monitor,

13 cruisers, 44 destroyers (one French), light vessels and 2,426 landing craft. The Western (American) zone had 3 battleships, 10 cruisers (two French), 35 destroyers, also frigates, corvettes and minesweepers and 1,700 LCs for forces O for Omaha, U for Utah and B for the follow-up division. The warships would also have a major role to play with their powerful artillery guns pounding the coastal defenses and even taking part in the land battle. A few instances of this: the population of Bayeux looked on with concern as navy shells passed over the town, landing in the Tilly area where a fierce battle was being fought. At the end of June 1944, an attempted counter-attack by II SS Panzer Corps was crushed by the Allied naval artillery.

Above : In the south of England, prior to D-Day, an LST loading a GMC truck through its bow door and access ramp. In this way, this type of ship could unload 500 tons of vehicles and equipment directly onto the beach. The landing craft we see alongside is an LCM.(US Navy).

Below : Plan of the beach sectors allocated to the two Allied armies; it took very strict organization to direct the thousands of vessels involved. (Heimdal).

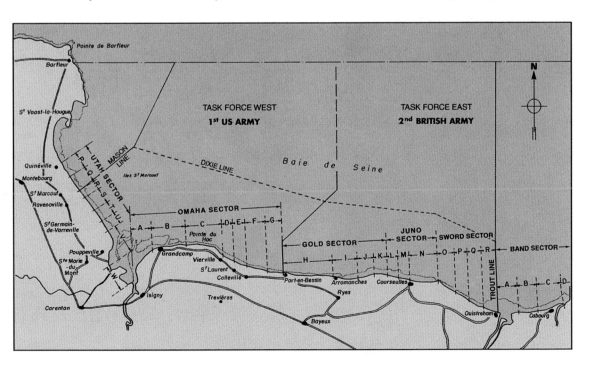

A line of LCIs heading for the Normandy coast. 265 of the two versions of this landing craft were used for Operation Overlord. (US Navy)

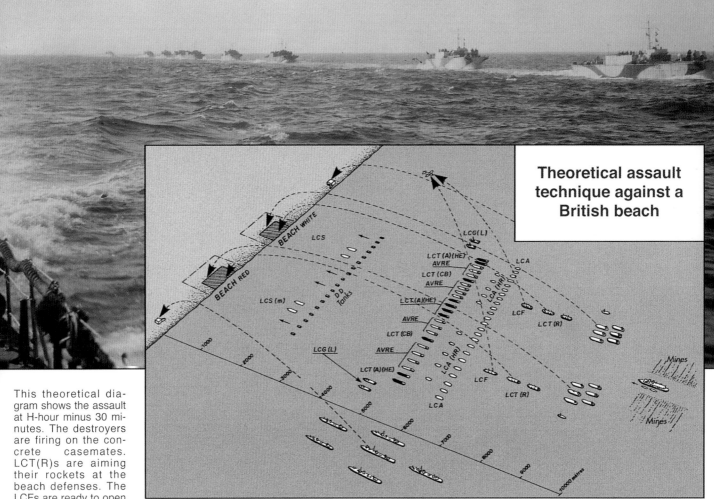

Theoretical assault technique against a British beach

BEACH WHITE
BEACH RED
LCS
LCS (m)
DD Tanks
LCG (L)
LCT (A)(HE)
LCA
LCG (L)
LCT (A)(HE)
AVRE
LCT (CB)
AVRE
LCT (A)(HE)
AVRE
LCT (CB)
AVRE
LCA (HR)
LCA (HR)
LCA (HR)
LCA
LCF
LCT (R)
LCF
LCT (R)
LCA
Mines
Mines
1000 2000 3000 4000 5000 6000 7000 8000 9000 10000 metres

This theoretical diagram shows the assault at H-hour minus 30 minutes. The destroyers are firing on the concrete casemates. LCT(R)s are aiming their rockets at the beach defenses. The LCFs are ready to open fire on any aircraft. The leading wave is approaching the coast with the LCSs carrying the assault infantry and DD tanks for their supporting fire. The AVRE tanks are coming in behind them.

Plan of the artificial harbor at Arromanches

1. Blockships
2. Phoenix caissons
3. Floating wharves
4. Intermediate wharf
5. Floating roadways
6. LST pier
7. Reinforced floating roadway
8. Liberty ship moorage
9. Coaster moorage
10. Moorage for shore forces vessels
11. Floating docks
12. Floating cranes
13. Munitions quay
14. Light "Rhino ferry" pontoon
15. "Swiss Roll" canvas floating roadway
16. Moorage for small landing craft
17. East channel
18. North channel
19. West channel
20. Service vessel shelter
21. Low tide mark
22. Row of bombardons

0   500   1000m

N

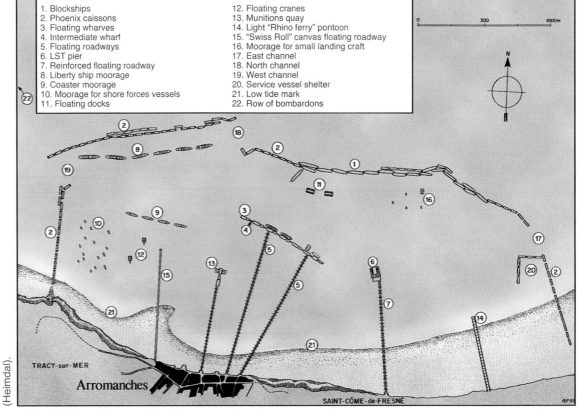

TRACY-sur-MER
Arromanches
SAINT-CÔME-de-FRESNÉ

(Heimdal).

The artificial harbors

The Normandy landing was also a race against time. The Allies had to bring as quickly as possible men, vehicles and equipment into the beachhead in order to gain overwhelming superiority over the Germans. Allied aircraft were to attack the German convoys to slow down their units coming up to the line and prevent reinforcements, fuel and ammunition from getting through. To bring ashore the wherewithal to ensure victory, the Allies, as we have seen, had an impressive armada of all kinds of vessels. But they needed to land men and equipment at a rapid, steady rate. Many naval units were able simply to beach their craft, send their load ashore over a mobile ramp, and sail off on the next tide. However, larger ships were also needed to bring in considerable tonnages, and the ports of Cherbourg, Le Havre and Dieppe could not be captured quickly enough. Under the impetus of Winston Churchill, a solution was found: artificial harbors.

This scheme posed a great many problems: very high tides (around 22 feet) powerful currents, frequent storms, transporting and then assembling the prefabricated elements.

The first thing to do was to carry out geological surveys to get an idea of the consistency of the future landing beaches, particularly those where the artificial harbors were to be set up. To do this, the Royal Navy sent over small squads to take samples under cover of night.

The artificial harbors - prefabricated harbors to be more precise - proved to be one of the Allies' most fantastic achievements, a veritable secret weapon. First requirement was a breakwater to shelter the inner harbor from the waves. These were the Phoenix caissons, blocks of hollow concrete, 70 m (over 200 ft) long, 15 m (50 ft) wide and 20 m (60 ft) high, as tall as an apartment building. With the bottom section filled with compressed air, they could be towed across the Channel by tug at a rate of three knots, and then set in position. They were built in 147 days by 20,000 laborers and engineers. 93 **bombardons** were also constructed to give extra protection to the harbor area. Floating quays

were also needed to berth the ships, with 33 **pier-heads** (built on the lines of oil rigs) which were mobile so as to ride on the tide, and 18 km (11 mi) of metal **floating roadways.** The whole arrangement was like a giant Meccano set!

Two harbors were designed. They were **Mulberry A** in the American sector at Saint-Laurent-sur-Mer, and **Mulberry B** in the British sector at Arromanches. The first Phoenix caisson arrived off Arromanches at dawn on June 9. By June 8, the two Mulberries were operational, and by June 12, 116,000 tons of supplies, 320,000 men and 54,000 vehicles had passed through the Arromanches Mulberry. The facilities were used by an average 280 ships per day. But on June 18, 19 and 20, the two artificial harbors were badly damaged in a heavy storm, with piers twisted, smashed to pieces or sunk, and bombardons set adrift. Such was the damage to the American Mulberry that it was closed for good and sections of it taken to Arromanches where huge efforts were needed to repair the second Mulberry, which finally remained in operation until December 1, 1944. In July 1944, its unloading capacity had reached 7,000 tons a day; meanwhile a daily average of 10,500 tons was being brought ashore on the beaches of the British sector and 35,000 tons on the beaches of the American sector.

Supremacy in the air

- Heavy bombers: 3,440
- Medium and light bombers: 930
- Fighters and fighter-bombers: 4,190
- Transport planes: 1,360
- Coastal Command: 1,070
- Reconnaissance: 520
- Rescue (sea and land): 80

These air forces were placed under the command of Air Chief Marshal Arthur Tedder, who had at his disposal 8th US Air Force, 9th US Air Force, RAF Bomber Command, RAF Coastal Command and 2nd Tactical Air Force.

In order to achieve such overwhelming superiority, the Allies started by conducting a war of attrition against the Luftwaffe (Pointblank directive), and their air raids over Germany left a great many German fighters concentrating on defending the Reich. To set the scene for a successful invasion, the Allied air force attacked communication lines, chiefly the railroads, so as to cut off supplies to the German troops. From February 9 to June 5, 1944, Allied aircraft carried out numerous operations in preparation for the landings. Starting at 18.30 hours on June 5, 1944, Operation Flashlamp targeted 10 heavy artillery batteries from Cherbourg to Le Havre with the bombs of 1,136 Allied four-engined aircraft. And during the night of June 5-6, a record 1,662 transport planes carried three airborne divisions over to Normandy: British 6th Airborne Division, US 82nd "All American" Airborne Division and US 101st "Screaming Eagles" Airborne Division. The 6,789 paratroops of this last division were taken over in 432 C-47s.

Above: The Typhoon was a formidable British fighter-bomber. It handled extremely well at low altitude, and had considerable fire power. (Model from the Bayeux museum).

1. Boeing B-17 F Flying Fortresses returning from a mission. These heavy bombers were flown by the 1st and 3rd bomber divisions of the Eighth USAAF, which had 2,000 heavy bombers and over 900 fighters. (US Air Force).

For Operation Overlord, the Allies had three trump cards: accurate intelligence regarding the German positions provided by the Resistance, a powerful fleet capable of landing thousands of men and supporting the operation with its heavy artillery, and an air force that enjoyed supremacy in the air.

Between June 5 and mid-August 1944, the Allies committed to the landing and Battle of Normandy the biggest ever concentration of aircraft, 11,590 planes and 3,500 gliders. On the other side, the Luftwaffe had just 210 fighters. On June 6, 1944, the Luftwaffe could only manage 319 sorties (including 121 involving fighters) against 14,000 by Allied aircraft, a superiority of 50 to 1 in the Allies' favor! On June 7, the Luftwaffe flew nearly 700 sorties over the Normandy front, and on June 10, it mustered 1300 aircraft in the west (including 475 fighters). The Allied aircraft were as follows:

At dawn on D-Day, Allied aircraft covered the landing beaches. 1,361 B-17s and B-24s took part in the preliminary operations, 1,083 other bombers dropping nearly 3,000 tons of bombs on 45 targets. Then all crossroads were crushed under bombs so as to slow down German reinforcements as they were moved up to the front. Coutances, Saint-Lô, Caen, Vire, Argentan, Lisieux, the destruction of the towns of Normandy began. Saint-Lô was almost completely wiped out, earning it the name "capital of the ruins". Such widespread destruction caused appalling damage, as well as heavy civilian casualties, for very little gain. On the other hand, the endless machine-gunning of the columns of German reinforcements, especially by the 2nd Tactical Air Force, was devastatingly effective, with the panzer columns sustaining heavy losses before they had even reached the front. They could only move up in any safety at night, but the June nights were very short. These divisions took many days to reach the front, turning the Battle of Normandy into a race against time to bring in reinforcements... Fuel supplies got through only with great difficulty. The panzers came in for merciless rocket attacks by the Allied fighter-bombers, a task in which the Typhoons performed outstandingly well. The panzers' worst enemies were not the Allied tanks but the planes. The German soldiers were terrified by the "Jabos" (their short name for the fighter-bomber) and it was the air force that decided the outcome of the Battle of Normandy.

2. A North American P-51 D Mustang, one of the best American fighter planes. (DAVA/Heimdal).

3. The North American B-25 Mitchell was an American medium bomber. (DAVA/Heimdal).

4. This RAF serviceman is lining up hundreds of Typhoon rockets at a field airstrip in Normandy. (IWM).

5. An American ground crew busy loading 12.7 bullets into the ammunition belts of a P-47's onboard machine-guns. The P-47 was a powerful US fighter used extensively during Operation Overlord. (DAVA/Heimdal coll.).

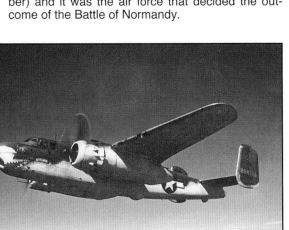

General Dwight D.Eisenhower
supreme Commander
Allied Expeditionary Forces

Lieutenant General
Omar Bradley
First US Army

UTAH

Lieutenant General
L. Collins
VII US Corps

OMAHA

Lieutenant General
L.T. Gerow
V US Corps

Major General
R.D. Barton
4th Infantry Division

Major General
R. Huebner
1st Infantry Division

Utah Beach

Major General
H. Gerhardt
29th Infantry Division

Sainte-Mère-Eglise

Major General
M. B. Ridgway
82nd Airborne Division

Omaha

Sainte-Marie-du-Mont

Major General
M.D. Taylor
101st Airborne Division

Air Chief Marshall
Arthur W. Tedder

Admiral
Bertram H. Ramsay

General
Bernard L. Montgomery
21st Army Group

Lieutenant General
Miles C. Dempsey
Second British Army

GOLD

Lieutenant General
C. Bucknall
XXX Corps

Lieutenant-General
John T. Crocker
I British Corps

Major General
Douglas A.H. Graham
50th British Infantry Division

JUNO

Major General
R.F.L. Keller
3rd Canadian Infantry Division

SWORD

Major-General
T.G. Rennie
3rd British Infantry Division

Gold Beach

Juno Beach

Sword Beach

Major-General
Richard N. Gale
6th Airborne Division

PEGASUS BRIDGE
RANVILLE

Pegasus the winged horse, emblem of 6th Airborne Division.

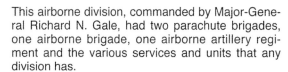

To cover the flanks of their five beach sectors, the Allies landed three airborne divisions in Normandy: two divisions of US paratroops in the Cotentin peninsula in the west, and one division of British paratroops in the east, between the Orne and Dives rivers: 6th Airborne Division.

6th Airborne Division

This airborne division, commanded by Major-General Richard N. Gale, had two parachute brigades, one airborne brigade, one airborne artillery regiment and the various services and units that any division has.

Each of the parachute brigades had three battalions of 600 paratroops each. The commander of 3rd Parachute Brigade was Brigadier James Hill. It comprised the 8th and 9th Battalions of the Parachute Regiment and also the 1st Canadian Parachute Battalion, and was dropped over the eastern flank. The 5th Parachute Brigade was commanded by Brigadier Nigel Poett. It comprised the 7th, 12th and 13th Battalions of the Parachute Regiment and was dropped over the Ranville sector in the west.

The 6th Airlanding Brigade (airborne infantry) included 2nd Ox and Bucks (minus Major Howard's D Company, which had been detached), the Devonshire Regiment's 12th Battalion and the Royal Ulster Rifles 1st Battalion. Each of the battalions were nearly a thousand-strong. The brigade was commanded by Brigadier Kindersley. The men were brought in by Horsa gliders carrying thirty men apiece.

The mission

On February 18, 1944, Major-General Gale received orders to provide support for the eastern flank of the Allied landing. 5th Parachute Brigade was to jump to the west of the Ranville sector, 3rd Brigade to the east towards the bridges over the Dives River, and the men of 6th Airborne Brigade would be committed to the south of the beachhead.

Major Howard, photographed in front of Pegasus Bridge in 1993. (Heimdal).

Metal beret insignia of the Ox and Bucks (Oxfordshire and Buckinghamshire Light Infantry).

The main mission was assigned to Brigadier Poett's 5th Brigade, briefed as follows by Major-General Gale: Your assignment is to capture and hold the bridges over the Caen canal and the Orne River, at Bénouville and Ranville, and to protect the Bénouville - Ranville - Bas de Ranville sector against infantry and armored attacks. It is of vital importance for the subsequent conduct of operations that the bridges should be secured intact. We are quite sure that the bridges are mined. The swiftness of the attack against the bridge defenses will be crucial. It will be carried out by a "coup de main" party of three airborne platoons brought over in gliders that will land as close to the target as is humanly possible. You must accept risks in carrying out this mission (Major Howard). The pathfinders who are to mark out the glider landing zones

1

1. Major General Richard N. Gale in front of his command post in Normandy, with the 6th Airborne Division pennant. (IWM).

Major General Richard N. Gale

Richard N. Gale was born in 1896. In 1915, he joined the Worcestershire Regiment, and later the machine-gun corps on the Western front in 1916, where he won the Military Cross. After the war, he continued his military career. In 1939, with the rank of major, he joined staff headquarters at the War Office in London. He commanded an infantry battalion from December 1940 to July 1941. In September 1941, following promotion to Brigadier General, he was put in command of a new unit, the 1st Parachute Brigade. He rose to Major General in 1943 and took command of 6th Airborne Division in April 1943.

He then subjected his division to intensive training, ensuring the collective spirit of his men, to have them fighting fit and ready to accomplish their mission. This they did successfully on June 6, 1944, returning to England in September. Major General Gale went on to command I British Airborne Corps, and later, in December 1944, became deputy commander of the First Allied Airborne Army. After the war was over until 1952, he received some important commands - command of the Rhine Army and of NATO's Army Group North. From 1957 to 1960, he was Allied deputy commander-in-chief in Europe. This general officer had strong personality, understood his men well, and was a real professional and leader of men. He died in London on July 29, 1982.

will jump at 00.20 hours. So the bridges must be secured by that time. Beyond the area between the two bridges, all the surrounding land is covered with poles connected by steel cables which make the landing zones unusable, so these will have to be cleared. The coup de main party will be followed immediately by a parachute drop which will consolidate the bridge positions and clean up the fields of all the obstacles in the way of the air landing. (...) You must launch your parachute force no more than thirty minutes after the coup de main party reaches the bridges. - 1st Special Service Brigade will cross the bridges at H + 4 (11.25) and you will be responsible for their safety along their line of advance in the paratroop sector. 6th Airlanding Brigade will land late on D-Day afternoon on your landing zone (N) and the zone cleared to the west of the canal (W), and you are responsible for Landing Zone N.

And while 5th Parachute Brigade was briefed to capture and hold Ranville, clear areas for the gliders, capture and hold the two bridges over the Orne River and the canal, 3rd Parachute Brigade was assigned two other tasks. Its 9th Battalion was to silence the Merville battery as Sword Beach came within range of its guns. Further east, 8th Battalion and 1st Canadian Battalion were to destroy bridges on the Dives, at Robehomme, Bures and Troarn, and prevent German reinforcements from getting through.

The coup de main party

As planned, Major John Howard was placed in command of the 150 men of 2nd Ox and Bucks D Company detailed to carry out the coup de main. They were to be brought over in six gliders each carrying 23 men of 2nd Ox and Bucks and five engineers. The first three gliders were to land near Bénouville Bridge (LZ-X) and the three others near Ranville Bridge (LZ-Y). The one was a bascule bridge, the other a swing bridge. Major Howard and Lieutenant Brotheridge with his n° 7 Platoon boarded glider n° 1, with Lieutenant Wood and his n° 2 Platoon in glider n° 2, and Lieutenant "Sandy" Smith and his n° 3 Platoon in the third glider. They were to land near Bénouville Bridge. Captain Brian Priday, the company's second-in-command, was in glider n° 4 to command the elements engaged against Ranville Bridge (glider n°s 4, 5 and 6).

The German forces

The sector was held by 711. Infanterie-Division under Generalleutnant Josef Reichert, (CP at Pont-l'Evêque) which had no more than a 40% static defense role. Also its elements were scattered. 21. Panzer-Divison on the other hand (CP at Saint-Pierre-sur-Dives) was located in the sector to the south of 6th Airborne Division's future dropping zone. On D-Day, under Major Hans von Luck, a battlegroup (Kampfgruppe Luck) was raised and committed against the airborne bridgehead. The only artillery position in the sector was the Merville battery (1./AR 1716), housing four 100mm Czech-built guns in casemates.

2

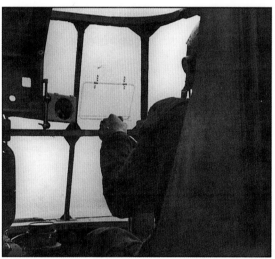

2. Alongside an Albemarle, pathfinders of 22nd Independent Parachute Company synchronize their watches. From l. to rt., De la Tour, Wells, Visher and Widwoop.

3. Operation Mallard on the evening of June 6: a pilot at the controls of a Horsa glider.

3 (Photos, IWM.)

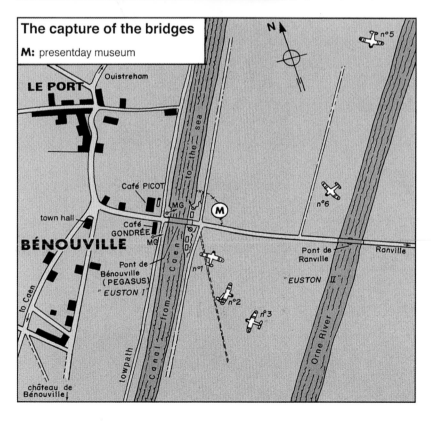

The capture of the bridges
M: presentday museum

Despite losses sustained in German counter-attacks, morale remained high among these paras photographed before Bréville on June 10. (IWM).

The capture of the bridges at Bénouville and Ranville

June 5 ended with the launch of Operation Tonga as 422 transport planes prepared to take off for Normandy with elements of 6th Airborne Division. Shortly before midnight, the leading convoy comprised only 38th Group aircraft, two Albemarles per Dropping Zone (DZ V, N, K) carrying pathfinders of 22nd Independent Parachute Company. A further 27 Albemarles and Halifaxes, six of them with six Horsas in tow carrying Major Howard's 170 men, joined this convoy carrying the men and heavy equipment needed to assist the main drop.

While the pathfinders were dropped to mark out the three DZs, the coup de main party in their six gliders approached their target just before midnight (one a.m. French time) in the first historic moments of June 6, 1944. Five of them landed according to plan near the two bridges. Glider n° 1 brought Major Howard to within 30 yards of the Bénouville bascule bridge. The assault was all over in five minutes; the few German guards were overpowered and the men of 2nd Ox and Bucks were already on the other side, however Lieutenant Brotheridge was killed. Across the water, the men from gliders 5 and 6 had captured the Ranville bridge. Glider n° 3 lost its way, landing 13 km (8 mi) further east. From Ranville, paratroops of 7th Battalion (Lieutenant-Colonel Pine-Coffin) arrived to reinforce the Ox and Bucks' bridgehead against German counter-attacks from the west and from Bénouville. Major Howard held out until Lord Lovat arrived with his commando brigade bang on time at around 13.00. Half an hour behind the first convoy, at 00.50, 110 Stirlings and Albemarles (38th Group) towing six Horsas, and 146 C-47s (46th Group) tugging 13 Horsas brought in the main elements, the divisional HQ, 2,600 paratroops from 5th Brigade (over DZ N) and 2,500 paratroops from 3rd Brigade (over DZ K and V). Shortly afterwards, the 1,200 men of divisional headquarters (artillery, engineers, medics) were dropped over DZ N.

But another two coup de main parties were in action too. These were assigned to the three other battalions of 3rd Brigade (Brigadier Hill).

Men of the Gordon Highlanders cross the bascule bridge at Bénouville, now known as "Pegasus Bridge", to join the east bank of the Orne River. This was a vital crossing point when fighting resumed north-east of Caen, particularly during Operation Goodwood on July 18, 1944. On the far bank we can see, from left to right, gliders n° 1 (Major Howard's) and n° 2. (IWM).

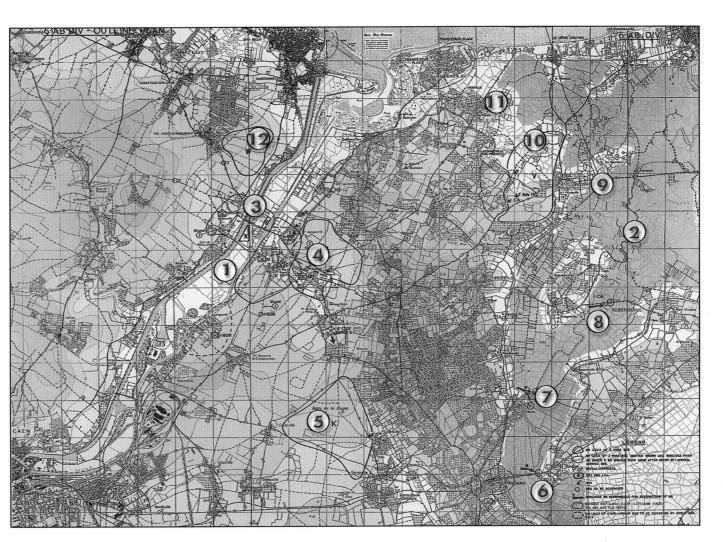

Merville and the bridges over the Dives

The pathfinders were dropped at 00.20 near the **Merville battery**, followed by Lieutenant-Colonel Otway's 9th Parachute Battalion, also in the battery sector (DZ V); but the men were well scattered and by **02.50** only 150 of the 600 paratroops who had been dropped had reached the muster point west of Varaville. Otway himself did not arrive until three in the morning. The battery was reached and a fierce battle ensued against the German artillery with IR 736 in reinforcement. The 22 German survivors surrendered, and the 100mm guns were silenced but not destroyed as only one glider had managed to bring in explosives, which was not enough. The paratroops lost 5 officers and 65 men killed or wounded. At 06.00, Otway and his men began to withdraw to Le Plein, their mission accomplished in part.

The **destruction of the bridges over the Dives** was a task assigned to the 3rd Brigade's two other battalions, 8th Parachute Battalion and 1st Canadian Parachute Battalion. Altogether there were five bridges to be destroyed. Using a system of locks, the Germans had inundated the low-lying and partly marshy Dives valley to the east of the airborne sector. However there were still roadways across this flooded area which could be taken by 711. Infanterie-Division reinforcements launching a counter-attack. This was the threat to the eastern flank of the Allied beachhead in Normandy that the destruction of the five bridges over the Dives was designed to remove. The battalions detailed to carry out this mission were dropped over DZ K at **00.50**. Six Horsa gliders landed on LZ K bringing in jeeps and explosives. The units mustered and set

off at approximately **02.30**. The paratroops were reinforced by the engineers of 3rd Para Squadron, with three platoons allocated to various targets. To the south, the 1st Platoon headed off for the **bridge at Troarn** with Major J. Rosevaere (Royal Engineers) and the paras of 8th Battalion. Rosevaere's jeep sped through Troarn with a trailer of explosives in tow under fire from the Germans. They reached the bridge and blew it up five minutes later. In the center, Lieutenant-Colonel Pearson (8th Battalion), 120 of his paratroops and the engineers of 3rd Para Squadron's 2nd Platoon, passed through Bavent on their way to the road and rail bridges at **Bures**. Captain Jukes led his assault group to these two objectives at **06.30**; the two bridges were duly demolished. Further north, with support from the engineers of 3rd Para Squadron's 3rd Platoon, 1st Canadian Parachute Battalion destroyed the bridges at **Robehomme** and **Varaville**, accomplishing their mission with very few casualties. Then all elements withdrew to defensive positions in the **Bavent** sector.

By three o'clock in the morning, Major-General Richard N. Gale was in charge at his HQ at Ranville, among his paratroopers of 5th Brigade (Brigadier Nigel Poett). The entire mission was a complete success and early in the afternoon, Lord Lovat's 1st Special Service Brigade arrived to reinforce the front to the north-east near **Amfreville**.

Finally, from **20.51** to **21.23**, Operation Mallard brought in more reinforcements of men of 6th Airlanding Brigade - the main body of 2nd Oxfordshire and Buckinghamshire Light Infantry (Ox and Bucks), one company of the 12th Devonshires and a battery.

1 The Orne with the canal to the west. **2** The Dives with the flooded marshlands to the east. **3** LZ X and Bénouville Bridge, LZ Y and Ranville Bridge. **4** Ranville and DZN for 5th Brigade. **5** LZK and DZK, to the south, for the gliders and reinforcements, and 3rd Brigade. **6** Troarn Bridge. **7** The Bures Bridges. **8** Robehomme Bridge. **9** Varaville Bridge. **10** Dropping Zone V. **11** Merville battery. **12** LZW, 6th Airlanding Brigade.

Lieutenant-Colonel Otway. (DR).

29

Sword Beach

Panoramic view of the beach at Riva-Bella/ Ouistreham in 1942. The position was then made up of six large bunkers each housing a 15.5 cm K18 (F) gun. It was further reinforced prior to the landing. We see the mouth of the Orne and in the background the coastal sectors of Merville and Houlgate. (BA).

Concrete beach obstacles still standing at Riva-Bella. (EG./Heimdal).

3rd Infantry Division and other units landed on June 6 across a narrow sector of beach (Queen White and Queen Red between Hermanville-sur-Mer and La Brèche d'Hermanville). While 1st Special Service Brigade, commanded by Lord Lovat, took Ouistreham before moving on to Bénouville to link up with the airborne bridgehead, the main body of 3rd Infantry Division headed off due south with Caen as their objective.

The German defenses

This sector was defended by elements of 716. Infanterie-Division (only 7,771 men on D-Day), commanded by Generalleutnant Wilhelm Richter, who then had his command post in the north of the city where the Caen Memorial now stands. He had just two infantry regiments at his disposal, Grenadier-Regiment 726 commanded by Oberst Walter Korfes, and Grenadier-Regiment 736 commanded by Oberst Ludwig Krug. These under-strength regiments were reinforced with battalions of eastern troops: Ost-Btl. 439 and 441 for the former, and Ost-Btl. 642 for the latter. The division's batteries were deployed along the coast some way inland.

The shoreline was defended by various resistance nests and strongpoints, but the artillery batteries were what caused the Allies the most trouble. On the east side of the mouth of the Orne, the Merville battery, Wn 01, had four casemates each holding a Czech-built 100mm gun; the Allies thought these casemates contained bigger guns liable to pose a threat to Sword Beach, which is why they launched an airborne operation against the battery (see chapter "Bénouville-Ranville").

Concrete shelters at what was Wn 17 (known to the Allies as "Hillman"); this position held up the British advance on D-Day. (EG/Heimdal).

A few strongpoints along the coast, Franceville (Stp. 05, Wn 06), La Pointe du Siège (Wn 07) and, across the Orne estuary, bring us to Ouistreham (Stützpunkt Caen 08) with a large artillery battery of six 155mm (French) guns in the concrete emplacements. Construction of the casemates to protect them had only just begun and, following air raids, the guns were unseated in May 1944. They were served by the men of 1./HKAA 1260 (formerly 1./HKAA 832). Overlooking the position was an imposing six-storey concrete Control bunker (now the Atlantic Wall Museum). Slightly to the rear, the water tower battery was served by the artillery of 716.ID (4./AR1716); it had four 155mm guns, again French, in bunkers.To the northeast, at Colleville, another battery (4./AR1716) was placed in casemates, it had rather less powerful guns: four 100mm (Czech-built) guns. Lastly, again near Colleville but a little to the rear, a powerful strongpoint, codenamed "Hillman" by the Allies and Wn 17 by the Germans, gave the British troops a hard time. Grenadier-Regiment 736 had its CP there.

3rd (British) Infantry Division

Under the command of Major General Tom G. Rennie since December 1943, this division was not a regional unit but was built up from battalions drawn from all over the country. Thus, the 8th Brigade comprised the 1st Suffolks (from SE England), the 2nd East Yorkshires (NE England) and the 1st South Lancashires (NW England). The 9th Brigade included the 2nd Lincolnshires (E England), the 1st K.O.S.B. (Scottish borders) and the 2nd R.U.R. (Ulster, Northern Ireland). The 185th Brigade comprised the 2nd Royal Warwickshires (Midlands), the 1st Royal Norfolks (E England), and the 2nd King's Shropshire Light Infantry (W England between Wales and Warwickshire). Through undecisiveness, this division was stopped short of Caen on D-Day and pinned down for a whole month, until July 8. On June 12, 1944, Major General T. G. Rennie was wounded and evacuated, to be replaced temporarily by the commanding officer of 8th Brigade, Brigadier E.E.E. Cass, and from June 23 by Maj. Gen. L.G. Whistler.

Major General Tom G. Rennie

Tom G. Rennie was born at Foochow in China in 1900. On leaving the Royal Military College at Sandhurst as a young officer, he was posted to the Black Watch, where he was appointed second-in-command of the 2nd Battalion. After following courses at Staff College in 1933 and 1934, he joined the 51st Highland Division which was engaged in France as part of the British Expeditionary Force. But Rommel made his lightning strike up to the Channel and he was taken prisoner at St Valéry in Normandy in June 1940, escaping just ten days later. He returned to England and the Black Watch, and fought in north Africa. He was awarded a DSO (Distinguished Service Order) for his action at El Alamein in 1942, and later took part in the Sicily campaign. In 1942 and 1943, he was put in command of 3rd Infantry Division. He prepared it for Overlord, but was later criticized for failing to training his unit to act quickly and press home their advantage in battle. On D-Day, he was held up by the German strongpoint codenamed "Hillman" and his hesitancy prevented him from taking Caen. On June 12, he broke his arm when his jeep hit a mine. On June 18, he was taken back to England and did not return to the continent until September 1944, when he took over command of 51st Highland Division, which he knew well. He was killed by a mortar shell on March 24, 1945, during the Rhine crossing.

Major General Tom G. Rennie. (IWM).

Badge of 3rd (British) Infantry Division

"Queen Red" sector, 08.42 on June 6. LCI 519 brings in the staff of 1st Special Service Brigade. In the foreground is Piper Bill Millin with his bagpipes, and on the column's right, Shimi Fraser of Lovat. (IWM).

The assault

At 05.47, HMS Frobisher opened fire on the beach at Ouistreham. The destroyers opened fire from 06.22 to 07.05, firing blind, but the more accurate rocket fire from the LCTs, LCGs and LCSs gave better results.

07.20. Day had dawned. The landing at Sword Beach was scheduled about 90 minutes later than on the other beaches, the German defenses were partly intact and the men of Grenadier-Regiment 736 were emerging from the deluge of fire. 22nd Dragoons' flail tanks were the first to hit the beach along with their squads of engineers. The leading AVREs arrived at 07.25. These powerful tanks engaged the enemy positions, then 31 amphibious tanks of 13/18th Royal Hussars arrived in turn to silence the 50 and 75mm guns. A good job well done by both tanks and engineers.

At 07.30, twenty LCAs brought in the assault companies: in the west 1st South Lancashire A and C Companies to Queen White; in the east 2nd East Yorkshire A and C Companies to Queen Red. But they were all held up at the top of the beaches behind the antitank wall. Then a flail tank knocked out a 75mm gun that had just caused 200 casualties among the East Yorkshires.

The two assault battalions' other companies and the two LCIs bringing in the Frenchmen of n°4 Commando (the Kieffer Commando) came ashore in turn at 07.31. After sprinting up the beach Commando n°4 opened a breach in the barbed wire. At 07.55, it was in the ruins of a holiday camp and headed off towards Ouistreham. At 08.42, LCI 501 hit the beach, the ramp was lowered, and to the sound of the bagpipes of Piper Bill Millin accompanying his commanding officer, Lord Lovat set off at the head of his 1st Special Service Brigade for the bridges held by the paratroops at Bénouville and Ranville.

At Ouistreham at around 09.30, the Frenchmen of the Kieffer Commando captured the casino, which had been turned into a bunker. At 10.00, Commando n° 4 reached the canal locks, which had not been mined. The main body of 1st Special Service Brigade carried on southwards along the Caen ship canal. At around 13.00, accompanied by Bill Millin and the French commandos and followed by the other commandos of the brigade, Lord Lovat joined Major Howard's men at Bénouville Bridge, thereby completing the link-up with the airborne bridgehead. Mission accomplished (see chapter "Bénouville-Ranville").

The men of 1st Suffolk reorganize on Queen White beach. The time: approximately 08.40. The man in the foreground is Peter Lucas, a member of a Beach Group. (IWM).

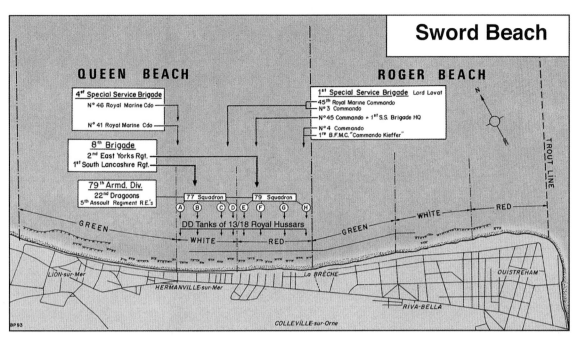

Lord Lovat's piper, Bill Millin. (IWM).

To the west, 3rd Infantry Division now had its 185th Brigade, which mustered in the north of Hermanville at 10.30. Two hours later, Brigadier Smith finally set off towards Caen with 600 men from three of his brigade's battalions. On the German side, no counter-attack had got underway so far. Most of the companies of 716. Infanterie-Division were in position along the coast, and most of them had been wiped out. Apart from strongpoint "Hillman", little remained to oppose the advance. The only armored reserve in the sector was made up of 21.Panzer-Division whose headquarters were at Saint-Pierre-sur-Dives and its tank regiment in that same sector, away from the coast. Although it did however have a few battalions in the Caen sector, the division was first committed against the airborne bridgehead east of the Orne, at 06.45. The decision to engage it north of Caen as well did not come through until 10.35. This led the

division to be arranged into three battlegroups; one (Kampfgruppe Luck) to fight the paratroops on the east bank of the Orne, the two others (Kampfgruppe Rauch and Kampfgruppe von Oppeln) to be committed on the west bank north of Caen, with orders to move up to the coast, near Lion-sur-Mer for KG Rauch, and between east of Lion and the mouth of the Orne for KG von Oppeln. Unfortunately they could not be engaged until 16.00! The Germans had no clear picture of their plight and their mobile forces were scattered. However, although for several hours 185th Brigade faced practically no further opposition, it failed to capitalize on the situation.

Lord Lovat

The legendary Simon Fraser Baron Lovat was born in 1911. His first name is often given the Scottish spelling, Shimi. The future seventeenth Baron Lovat spent his childhood at Beaufort Castle in Scotland. His remote ancestors from Anjou, the lords of La Fréselière, who came over with the Norman barons, came to be called Frisel (Simon Frisel was a Scottish lord in 1160), then Fraser. Shimi Fraser became an officer with the Scots Guards in 1932. On his father's death in 1933 he became seventeenth Baron Lovat and twenty-fifth head of the Fraser clan. When war broke out, he was a captain and volunteered for the Lovat's Scouts, a unit formed by his father in 1899. He joined n° 4 Commando and in March 1941 took part in the successful raid on the Lofoten Islands. In August 1942, Shimi Fraser of Lovat was promoted to Lieutenant-Colonel and commander of n° 4 Commando, leading that unit on the unsuccessful Dieppe raid. On the eve of Overlord, he was placed in command of 1st Special Service Brigade comprising three army commandos (n°s 3, 4 and 6), and n° 45 Royal Marine Commando. His mission, along with 6th Airborne Division, was to hold the left flank of the Allied beachhead. His brigade landed at Sword Beach and linked up with the airborne bridgehead as reinforcement. This finally made a legendary figure of him. Shimi Fraser of Lovat died in Scotland on the banks of the Beanly on March 16, 1995.

Lord Lovat.

Left: The Riva Bella/Ouistreham Control bunker was a concrete tower overlooking the whole sector. Nowadays it is home to an interesting museum devoted to the Atlantic Wall. (EG/Heimdal).

Missed opportunities

The Colleville garrison surrendered at 13.00, but "Hillman" held out until about 22.00. At 13.30, Caen came under heavy bombardment, the start of a long agony for the great Norman town. The ridge at Périers-sur-

le-Dan was finally reached at **15.00.** At around 15.15, KSLI and some antitank guns followed towards Beuville. Progress was careful and finally 21.Panzer-Division launched an armored counter-attack from Lebisey at about **16.20.** The panzers of KG von Oppeln sustained British antitank gun fire from Biéville and were kept in check. KG Rauch on the other hand found a way through between the troops that had come ashore at Juno Beach and those landing at Sword Beach and it was around 20.00 when six Panzer IVs from this battlegroup finally reached the coast. However, at 21.00, the German party was passed overhead by 250 aircraft towing gliders bringing in reinforcements to the Ranville sector as part of Operation Mallard. Faced with this threat, KG Rauch quickly withdrew. The front then stabilized north of Caen for a month, particularly as a second armored division, 12. SS-Panzer-Division "Hitlerjugend", also arrived on the scene, launching a counter-attack north-west of Caen on June 7. Thus two panzer divisions contrived to stand in the way of two Allied divisions, 3rd Canadian Infantry Division and 3rd British Infantry Division, for a month of fierce fighting, until July 8, 1944.

7

The Allied advance in the Sword Beach sector

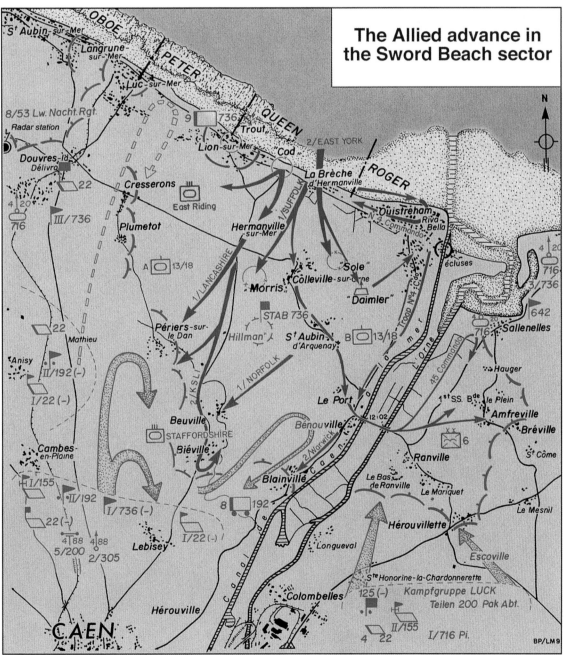

1. Insignia worn on their berets by the Frenchmen of Commando n° 4, the "Kieffer Commando". (Heimdal).

2. Hermanville-la-Brèche, during the afternoon of June 6. The platoon protecting 9th Infantry Brigade HQ advances westward, passing by the Hôtel de la Brèche. Here we see a Bren-gun carrier belonging to 33rd Field Artillery Rgt. (IWM).

3. The same spot today, the Place du Cuirassé Courbet. (EG/Heimdal).

4. The Australian war correspondent Chester Wilmot talking with French commandos (Commando n° 4), photograph taken at Amfreville on June 9, 1944. (IWM).

5. The men in the platoon protecting 9th Infantry Brigade HQ advance towards the square seen in the first photograph; on the left, we recognize the back of the Hôtel de la Brèche. (IWM).

6. The same view today. (EG/Heimdal).

7. A Panzer-IV of 21. Panzer-Division is launched on a counter-attack but these tanks did not line up until late afternoon on D-Day, too late to threaten the landing of British troops. Their presence did however prevent 3rd (British) Infantry Division from reaching Caen that day. (BA).

One of the Merville battery casemates stormed by paratroops of 6th Airborne Division.

Below: Ouistreham/Riva-Bella. The Atlantic Wall Museum is housed in the imposing concrete tower of the control bunker overlooking the beach.

5

IST BN THE SUFFOLK REGIMENT

IN MEMORY OF THOSE WHO FELL ON 6TH JUNE 1944 IN THE LIBERATION OF
COLLEVILLE SUR ORNE, THE CAPTURE OF "HILLMAN" AND LATER DURING
FIGHTING IN NORMANDY AND NORTH WEST EUROPE.
THANKS TO THE GENEROSITY OF A COLLEVILLE FAMILY THIS SITE RECORDS
FOR FUTURE GENERATIONS THE BRAVERY AND SACRIFICE OF THESE SOLDIERS.

A LA MÉMOIRE DE CEUX QUI TOMBÈRENT LE 6 JUIN 1944 POUR LA LIBÉRATION
DE COLLEVILLE SUR ORNE, POUR LA PRISE DE "HILLMAN" ET ENSUITE AU COURS
DE LA BATAILLE DE NORMANDIE ET DANS LE NORD OUEST DE L'EUROPE.
GRÂCE A LA GÉNÉROSITÉ D'UNE FAMILLE DE COLLEVILLE, CET ENDROIT RAPPELLERA
AUX GÉNÉRATIONS FUTURES LA BRAVOURE ET LE SACRIFICE DE CES SOLDATS.

Above: The "Hillman" position which slowed down the advance of 3rd Infantry Division is open to visitors. Here we see a plaque in memory of the men of the Suffolk Regiment who fought here.

Left: Facing the Ouistreham/Riva-Bella casino, a museum is devoted to Sword Beach and to the Frenchmen of Commando n° 4.

Below: A Centaur tank on display near Pegasus Bridge at Bénouville.

Above: The British cemetery at Ranville, where many paratroopers of 6th Airborne Division are buried.

Right: The Ranville cemetery. Grave of a British paratrooper killed on D-Day.

(Photos, Erik Groult/ Heimdal)

Juno Beach

Major General Rod F.L. Keller, commander of 3rd Canadian Infantry Division which landed at Juno Beach on June 6, 1944. (PAC).

Cloth badges of 3rd Canadian Infantry Division sewn onto the top of the sleeve.

The Canadians in the middle of the British battle order

Juno Beach, in the middle of the British sector, had a crucial role to play on June 6. With 10 km (6 mi) of beaches, it formed the link between the Sword and Gold sectors. As part of I British Corps under Lieutenant General J.T. Crocker, who was also supervising Sword, the powerful 3rd Canadian Infantry Division was to land on this section of beach.

Major General Rod F.L. Keller

Rod Keller was born in 1900 at Tetbury, in England. His family then emigrated to Canada where he joined the Royal Military College (RMC) in 1920. Having been promoted to captain in 1925, he rejoined the RMC in 1928 until 1932. His round face and physical strength earned him the nickname of Captain Blood. After training at Staff College he became a staff officer. In June 1941 he took command of his first regiment, Princess Patricia's Canadian Light Infantry (PPCLI). Six weeks later he was promoted to the rank of brigadier and took over command of 1st Canadian Infantry Brigade. His next promotion was to major general in 1942, when he took command of 3rd Canadian Infantry Division.

Although Lieutenant General Crerar had spoken very highly of him, his superiors felt he was not quite up to the tasks ahead. This was somewhat borne out by the facts, and the question of relieving him of his command was actually raised. After the excitement of the landings, Major General Keller lost his nerve. However, General Montgomery hesitated to dismiss a Canadian general who was still popular with his men. Fate however took a hand and he was very badly wounded on August 8, 1944 when American bombs fell short of their target. He died of a heart attack in Caen in 1954 during celebrations marking the 10th anniversary of the Normandy landing.

Cap insignias and shoulder flashes

7th brigade
1. Canadian Scottish.
2. « Reginas ».
3. Winnipegs (« Little black Devils »).

9th Brigade
4. « Novas ».
5. HLI.
6. « Glens ».

3rd Canadian Infantry Division

This division, with a strength of three infantry brigades, was commanded by Major General Rod F.L. Keller. Each brigade comprised three battalions, the equivalent of a German regiment at full strength.

7th Brigade (Brigadier Harry W. Forster) included the "Little Black Devils" of the Royal Winnipeg Rifles (Lieutenant Colonel John M. Meldram), the "Johns" of the Regina Rifle Regiment (Lieutenant Colonel Foster M. Matheson), and the Canadian Scottish (1st Battalion - Lieutenant Colonel F.N. Cabeldu), the "Scots".

8th Brigade (Brigadier K.G. Blackader) included the Queen's Own Rifles of Canada (Lt-Col Spragge) - the Queen's - a French-speaking regiment, the Régiment de la Chaudiere (Lt-Col Paul Mathieu), and the North Shore (New Brunswick) Regiment (Lt-Col D.B. Buell).

9th Brigade (Brigadier D.G. Cunningham), a Scottish brigade comprising the Highland Light Infantry (HLI - Lt-Col. F.M. Griffiths), the Stormont Dundas and Glengarry Highlanders (SDGH, Lt Col G.H. Christiansen), and the North Nova Scotia Highlanders (NNSH, Lt Col Charles Petch).

This Canadian division was also accompanied by the usual support and service units:

- Recce group: 17th Duke of York's Royal Canadian Hussars (7th Reconnaissance Regiment);

- Machine guns: Cameron Highlanders of Ottawa (M.G.). They were shared among the infantry battalions;

- Field artillery: 12th, 13th, 14th and 19th Royal Canadian Artillery (RCA)

- Antitank: 3rd Antitank Regiment;

- Engineers: 5th, 6th, 16th and 18th Companies (Royal Canadian Engineers);

In addition, this well-armed and fully motorized division was supported by an independent tank brigade that was attached to it. With this reinforcement, the motorized infantry division had more firepower than a German panzer division (about 18,000 men for the infantry division and a further 3,500 for the tank brigade).

(Musée Mémorial de Bayeux collection/Photos by Heimdal)

The German defenses

As with the Sword sector, the Juno sector allocated to the Canadian division offered a low shoreline with no natural obstacles. From east to west, it covered four villages and as many major strongpoints. These were big, densely populated coastal villages with narrow streets. **Saint-Aubin** was defended by Wn 27 - just one small casemate housing a 50mm gun covering both sides of the seafront (still complete with its gun). **Bernières,** where the main feature was the tall Gothic church steeple which made a good lookout post, was defended by Wn 28 - one casemate with an antitank gun, another with a 50mm gun, and several concrete shelters. 5/IR 736 had its command post in the locality. Further west, the mouth of the River Seulles was strongly defended by two positions. On the east bank, **Courseulles** was defended by Wn 29, with a

At the start of the war, the Canadian Army was made up of just a nucleus of 5,000 servicemen of every rank, and a 50,000-strong militia. But during the Battle of Normandy the Canadians hardened into experienced fighters, its strength growing to as many as 600,000 officers and men.

casemate for an 88mm gun and two more, each containing a 75mm gun. Also along the quayside there was a 50mm gun (still in place) covering access to the harbor channel. On the other bank, Wn 31 was set in the dunes up from the oyster beds with an observation post under an armored bell, a casemate with machine-guns, and two 50mm guns, one of which was in a casemate controlling the west bank of the harbor channel. The company defending the sector, 6./IR 736, had its command post sited in a concrete bunker. The fourth village, **Graye**, was a little to the rear. The harbor entrance was so strongly defended as it controlled access to the only port between Ouistreham and Port-en-Bessin.

3rd Canadian Infantry Division was tasked to land 7th Brigade on "Mike" beach (Courseulles and Graye), and 8th Brigade on "Nan" beach (Bernières) with support from 48th RM Commando (British) to the east at Saint-Aubin. It was to reach and cross Highway 13 as far as the Paris-Cherbourg railroad ("Ork" line) and capture the airfield at Carpiquet - no easy assignment.

4

NORTH . NOVA . SCOTIA HIGHLANDERS

5

HIGHLAND LICHT INFANTRY CANADA

Below: A casemate at Wn 27 housing a 50mm (KwK L/42 5 cm) gun still in position at Saint-Aubin-sur-Mer. (E. Groult/Heimdal).

6

GLENGARRIANS CANADA

Captain Gordon Brown replaced Major Love who was killed on the beach at Courseulles at the head of the Regina Rifle Regt.'s D Company. (G. Bernage coll.).

Juno Beach Landing

07.45. 7th Brigade came ashore on either side of the mouth of the Seulles. To the east, opposite Courseulles, on "Nan Green", the DD tanks of 1st Hussars B Squadron lowered their skirts as they emerged from the waves, coming in ahead of the Regina A and B Companies (Majors Grosch and Peters respectively). But in such heavy seas, 13 amphibious tanks, including Major Duncan's, capsized during the 5 km (3 mi) run-in. Only 14 of them reached the beach, with Sergeant Leo Gariepy's tank Bucéphale leading the way. The tanks immediately opened fire on the German positions, enabling B Company to seize these positions. On the right, all the tanks that were supposed to support A Company sank. A casemated 75mm gun held out until 09.45, when it was knocked out with the help of a Royal Marines Centaur tank's 95mm howitzer. Major Grosch was wounded, Captain Shawcross taking his place in command of Regina Rifles A

Company. Two companies of this regiment followed up: C Company (Major Tubb) and D Company (Major Love, who was killed on the beach, to be replaced by Captain Gordon Brown). Mines inflicted heavy losses on D Company on the beach, leaving just 49 survivors. Courseulles was divided into 12 zones and soon cleared.

West Royal Winnipeg Rifles were preparing to land on Mike beach opposite the village of Graye when a mortar shell hit an LCA offshore, killing 20. B Company on the left and A Company on the right reached the beach but were supported by only a few tanks of 1st Hussars A Squadron, the rest having capsized. Shellfire destroyed the last DD tanks, and B company sustained heavy losses; the "Little Black Devils" mustered in the dunes, where they had to wait until 11.00 for support to arrive from tanks landing directly on the beach. Further west, by keeping out of the shellfire from the casemates, D Company had fewer losses. It moved forward to Graye and mopped up. Still further west, 1st Canadian Scottish C Company was brought ashore to capture a casemate, which it did. It then proceeded to the Graye sanitarium.

To the east, 8th Brigade came ashore at **08.05** with the Queen's Own Rifles of Canada at "Nan White" opposite Bernières. They suffered heavy casualties as the DD tanks were unable to follow, leaving the infantry to fend for themselves. Major H.E. Dalton's A Company landed opposite the train station and the "Norman house" they were using as landmarks. The men quickly clambered over the concrete sea wall. But on the left, B Company landed near a strongpoint codenamed "Cassine" by the Canadians, losing 2/3 of its men and all its officers to the machine-guns and the two 50mm guns of this redoubt. The position was eventually silenced by three infantrymen with grenades. The sector was cleared at 09.30, but the regiment's two reserve companies (C and D) had all their LCAs damaged by beach obstacles, and the men had to swim ashore. Then came the tanks of the Fort Garry Horse. In a second wave, the French Canadians of

The landing at Bernières-sur-Mer. (PAC).

Right: 7th Brigade came ashore with two companies of the Royal Winnipeg Rifles and one company of 1st Canadian Scottish at Graye-sur-Mer, with tanks of the 1st Hussars in support. (Heimdal map).

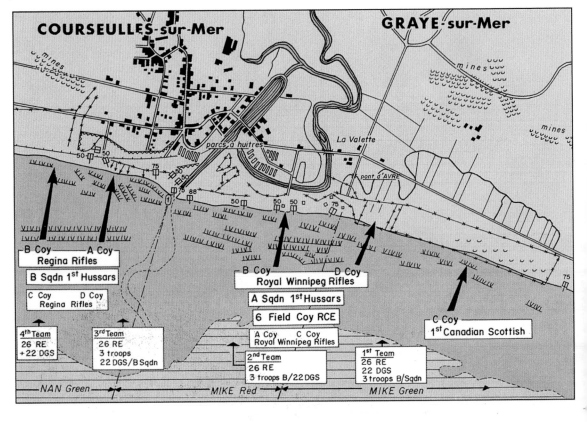

40

Left: Saint-Aubin-sur-Mer. A 50mm gun still in place in its concrete converging at this corner. (Photo E. Groult/Heimdal).

1. Progress through Saint-Aubin-sur-Mer by the Canadian North Shore Regt. (Heimdal map).

2. Just after the landing, one of the casemated guns that had been threatening the beach at Courseulles. (PAC).

3. Wn 28 at "Cassine". This strongpoint had two antitank guns; this photograph shows a casemate with a machine-gun nest. (PAC).

Régiment de la Chaudière completed mopping-up operations at Bernières, where the local population were amazed to hear them speaking French.

At **07.55** the North Shore Regiment landed in the western sector of Saint-Aubin. A Company, to the west, with the DD tanks of Fort Garry Horse in support, met with little opposition, reaching its first objective at 09.50 for the loss of only 24 men. Further east, opposite the village, B Company came under fire from Wn 27. This position was finally outflanked to the west through a maze of streets blocked by obstacles. With their tanks, the Fort Garry Horse eventually captured the position, counting 50 German dead. The British commandos of 48th Royal Marines Commando had followed up on the left wing of this regiment at **08.10** to neutralize the beach defenses. Of the 630 men brought ashore, by evening the unit was down to 341 unwounded men. The Churchill "Petards" launched a successful attack on the casemates. The last strongpoint fell at 11.30 under fire from the Royal Marines Centaur tanks and assaults by the Commandos. It took another 24 hours to mop up at Saint-Aubin.

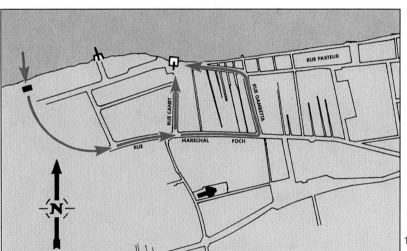

The Canadian advance

The first objective, the coastal strip, had been achieved with heavy losses especially opposite Graye, where the Royal Winnipeg Rifles recorded 128 casualties, including 55 killed. The Regina Rifle Regiment suffered 108 losses at Courseulles including 42 dead. 1st Canadian Scottish had 87 casualties, 21 of which were fatal. The Queens Owns had 7 officers killed and 69 wounded at Bernières. The total for Juno Beach was 319 dead, 528 wounded and 45 taken prisoner. The Canadians had now to reach the intermediate "Elm" line.

In the west, after capturing Vaux Castle (Graye sanitarium) with grenades, the Canadian Scottish joined the Winnipegs who were facing stout resistance at Sainte Croix on emerging from a marshy area (where an AVRE capsized) and clearing Graye. The Canadian Scottish and Winnipegs joined forces again at Colombiers-sur-Seulles and beyond Pierrepont where they stopped for the evening after crossing the "Elm" line, but still out of reach of Highway 13 and the "Ork" line and having actually withdrawn from Le Fresne-Camilly.

In the center, starting from Courseulles, the Regina Rifles with A Company reached Reviers at 15.00. Lieutenant Colonel Matheson faced stronger resistance than expected east of the Seulles river, from antitank guns near Reviers. He only reached Fontaine Henry in the evening, barely halfway to his objective.

To the east, 8th Brigade had to move inland as quickly as possible to allow the reserve 9th Brigade to land and advance in its turn. Major General Keller was still on board HMS "Hilary" as his two brigades started to move in. He tried to get an accurate picture of how the situation was progressing, with everything hinging on those decisive hours. In view of the situation, he chose to land the 9th Brigade on Bernières beach. But at the time he did not know about the congestion on the beach, as the Royal Navy had not told him they had just closed "Nan Red" beach at Saint-Aubin! Bottlenecks at the beach exits soon proved a major headache for the Allies on D-Day, with thousands of vehicles pouring onto the mainland all at once. 9th Brigade, which had a crucial role to play, landed at 11.30 at Bernières on a beach still overcrowded with the men and vehicles of 8th Brigade. War correspondent Ross Munroe, who was there, wrote of the chaos the 9th Brigade landing started

Despite sustaining heavy losses on the beaches, the Canadian brigades penetrated inland and reinforcements were brought ashore. Here we see some DD tanks on the left, and barrage balloons placed overhead to foil any attempted attacks by enemy aircraft. (PAC).

in, with roads chock full of impatient soldiers keen to push on ahead, and how fortunately the Germans failed to bomb the locality.

Major General Rod Keller in turn came ashore at Bernières at **12.45**. He was accompanied by several officers, among them Brigadier R.A. Wyman, commander of 2nd Armored Brigade. General Keller then realized the scale of the confusion and immediately ordered a rapid advance, but German resistance had stiffened in places, slowing down the Canadian advance. 8th Brigade was also held up as too were the North Shores at Tailleville, near Douvres radar station, a pocket of German resistance which held out for a whole week behind the Allied lines. General Keller was furious about these traffic jams and delays, but he had first to mop up these pockets of German resistance. Meanwhile, his intelligence officers warned him of a possible intervention by 21. Panzer-Division and 12. SS-Panzer-Division late in the afternoon.

9th Brigade did not get out of Bernières till 16.00, moving on to Bény-sur-Mer. They carried on as far as Anguerny with the Novas who eventually reached Villons-les-Buissons at **20.00**. The Novas were the spearhead of the Canadian advance, and were only 5 km (3 mi) away from Carpiquet airfield when they were ordered to stop for the night like all other units. Yet there was nothing ahead of them, the German front had been blasted away! Lieutenant McCormick of 1st Hussars actually crossed Highway 13 unopposed with his Sherman tank group, coming within view of the hangars at Carpi-

Left: Among the soldiers there were some French Canadians, which made it easier to fraternize with the civilian population. Here Micheline Grave and other women chat with Canadian soldiers at Bernières-sur-Mer. (PAC).

quet. German reinforcements had been held up in the confusion which still prevailed at German High Command level and the Allied air forces had also been highly effective in slowing down the Germans on their way up to the front line.

D-Day losses:

7th Brigade: 323 casualties, including 118 fatal
8th Brigade: 373 casualties, including 110 fatal.

On **June 7**, 7th Brigade reached and crossed Highway 13, the Winnipegs at Putot, the Reginas at Bretteville and Norrey. 9th Brigade advanced towards Carpiquet but came under frontal attack at Authie by a battlegroup of 12. SS-Panzer-Division that had just arrived at Ardenne Abbey that morning. The brigade suffered heavy losses in the face of the panzers' firepower, and fell back to Buron.

On **June 8**, 7th Brigade was attacked from east to west towards Bretteville l'Orgueilleuse by a battlegroup led by SS-Standartenfuhrer (SS Colonel) Kurt Meyer with two Panther tank companies in support. The Reginas were entrenched in Bretteville and Norrey, and 12. SS-Panzer-Division's night attack was a failure. However, following a stiffening of the German defense, the front made no further progress for almost a month, with fierce fighting on both sides.

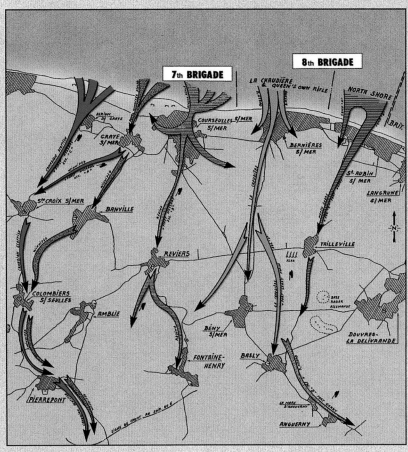

Above: Advances inland up to midnight on June 6. (Heimdal map).

Bernières-sur-Mer. Mopping up in the village was completed by 09.30. German prisoners were rounded up under the antitank wall. We can see one of the "Cassine" casemates. (PAC).

Below: The same site as it is today. (E. Groult/Heimdal).

1. Bernières-sur-Mer, Canadian soldiers of the Queen's Own Rifles have just captured Wn 28, "Cassine", one casemate with a 50mm gun is visible here. This strongpoint had two of these guns and they were the cause of heavy casualties sustained by Major Dalton's B Company, which lost 65 men on the beach. (PAC).

2. The same site as it is today. (EG/Heimdal).

3. Another view of this casemate which has been turned into a commemorative monument. (EG/Heimdal).

4. Churchill A.V.R.E. at Graye-sur-Mer. (EG/Heimdal).

5. Sherman DD tank at Courseulles-sur-Mer. (EG/Heimdal).

6. The Lorraine Cross at Graye-sur-Mer marks the spot where General de Gaulle landed on June 14 1944. (EG/Heimdal).

7. Canadian monument at Courseulles-sur-Mer. (EG/Heimdal).

8. Monument to the Régiment de la Chaudière at Bernières-sur-Mer. (EG/Heimdal).

Gold Beach

Major General D.A.H. Graham, commander of 50th Infantry Division. (IWM).

50th Infantry Division shoulder flash with its two Ts (Musée Mémorial de Bayeux/Heimdal).

The mission of XXX Corps under Lieutenant General C. Bucknall was to come ashore across five kilometers (3 mi) of beach between Asnelles (Le Hamel) and Ver-sur-Mer, capture Bayeux after linking up on the left (eastwards) with the Canadians and with the Americans on the right, and then advance towards Tilly-sur-Seulles, south of Bayeux. This sector was codenamed Gold Beach. XXX Corps had the strength of three divisions: 50th (Northumberland) Division commanded by Major General D. Graham, 7th Armored under Major General George W.E.J. Erskine, and 49th (West Riding) Division under Major General E.H. Barker. Two brigades (56th Infantry, and 8th Armored), elements of 79th Armored Division and some corps units made up the rest of the force. British 50th Infantry Division was to land at Gold Beach with 56th Infantry Brigade following up.

50th Infantry Division

The British 50th Infantry Division was theoretically a division recruited in the northeast of England, hence the name Northumbrian, Northumbria being the area colonized by the Danes - the "Danelaw". The divisional insignia of two interlocking red T's on a black background refer to the rivers Tyne and Tees which flow through the area on the way to the North Sea. The Tyne flows through Northumberland and Newcastle-upon-Tyne and the Tees slightly further south through County Durham and Middlesbrough. The division was composed of three infantry brigades - 151st Brigade, with three

infantry battalions from the Durham Light Infantry, 6th, 8th and 9th who were recruited in County Durham, named for its see at Durham Cathedral, a superb example of medieval architecture dating back to Norman times. 69th Brigade was another unit of northerners, as the 5th East Yorkshires, the 6th Green Howards and the 7th Green Howards were recruited in the neighboring county of Yorkshire. On the other hand the 231st Brigade under Brigadier Stanier was recruited mainly in southern England with its three battalions, the 2nd Devonshires, 1st Hampshires and 1st Dorsetshires recruited from counties along the southern coast of England: Devon (capital Exeter), Hampshire (Southampton and Winchester), and Dorset (Bournemouth). However, regional battalions were mixed after the First World War after being almost completely annihilated in the battles on the western front, making widows of most of the women from the community where the men were recruited. From then on units recruited men from anywhere in the United Kingdom to prevent such a thing happening again. Battle losses also diluted the regional makeup of units.

In the lead-up to Overlord, the "Fifty Div" had already won its spurs in north Africa in 1942 at Gazala and El Alamein. In its ranks were coalminers, or Geordies as northeasterners are called, reputedly stubborn fighters. The division distinguished itself for the way it stood its ground under fire on Gold Beach and later in battle in the Tilly-sur-Seulles sector.

Emblem of the Green Howards Regiment on the monument at Crépon. (GB/Heimdal).

May 29, 1944. Soldiers of the Green Howards Regiment (50th Inf. Div.) boarding SS Empire Lace. (IWM).

Major General D.A.H. Graham

Cutting a forbidding mustachioed figure, Douglas A.H. Graham was 51 in 1944. He was born in 1893 and soon after the start of World War One he joined the Cameronians, also called the Scottish Rifles, a unit recruited in western Scotland. He ended the war with the rank of captain, having been awarded the Military Cross and the French Croix de Guerre. He stayed in the army and served in Palestine from 1936 to 1939 where he was put in command of a regiment. He was a dour Scot from the lowlands, with indomitable courage and deep religious convictions. He took an independent and practical view of military matters and did not let himself be carried away by theory and intellectual conceptions. He proved to be an ideal leader during moments of crisis. When war broke out with Italy, he joined the army in North Africa and served with distinction in the desert war, was awarded the DSO and Bar and given command of the 56th (London) Infantry Division. He then served in the Italian campaign and was wounded at Salerno. After convalescing in England, he was placed in command of 50th Infantry Division, which he trained for Overlord.

On June 6, he landed at about noon and set up his command post at Meuvaines where he waited to be relieved by the 7th Armored Division which followed him ashore. His many successes earned him further decorations. He retired from the army in 1947 and died in Scotland in 1971.

Attached to the 50th Division was 56th Independent Infantry Brigade, made up of three infantry battalions, the 2nd South Wales Borderers, the 2nd Gloucestershire Regt (2nd Glosters for short), and the 2nd Essex Regt.

The German defenses

Gold Beach was a sector of low flat beaches with high bluffs at either end. To the east the village of **Ver-sur-Mer** which extends to a plateau rising to about 35m (115ft). The beach was defended by Wn 33 in a flanking casemate equipped with an 88mm gun and two further positions each with a 50mm gun manned by IR 736's 7th Company. Higher up, the village of Ver-sur-Mer was flanked by another pair of artillery batteries. In the west, near the lighthouse was **Mont-Fleury battery** (Wn 35a) served by 3./HKA 1260. The casemates, which were equipped with four 122mm ex-Russian guns, had not been completed. South-east of the village, **Mare-Fontaine battery** was served by 6./AR 1716 (716. ID gunners) with 100mm guns in casemates. Inland a third battery installed to the S.W. at Crépon (Wn 35b) completed the system; it was served by 5./AR 1716.

mountain gun and westwards by Wn 44 on the Tracy cliff with a 47mm casemated gun. Beyond, between Arromanches and Port-en-Bessin, the **Longues** naval battery (4./HKAA 1260) under Oberleutnant MA Kurt Weil served the four mighty 150mm guns in their casemates on the cliff top.

1. Wn 36, west of Asnelles, had a small casemate for a 50mm gun still visible today.
2. One of the casemates of the Mare-Fontaine battery, fitted with 100mm guns.
Background photograph: a casemate from what was Wn 37 at Asnelles.
(Photos, E. Groult/Heimdal).

West of Ver-sur-Mer stretched a flat coastline, behind which was a wide marsh which acted as a natural barrier before the plateau extending eastwards and the plain to the west. The sandy dunes at **Hable de Heurtot** were defended by Wn 35, a unit of Russians enlisted in the Wehrmacht, 3./441. Their task was to defend a difficult pathway across the marshes.

After this part of the coast the rest was much easier going, but much more heavily defended coming into **Asnelles**. Wn 36 at Les Roquettes blocked the route with a 50mm gun in a pillbox and a casemate equipped with machine guns. In the center, at Le Hamel, Wn 37 equipped with a casemated 75mm gun barred the way. Further west, Wn 38 had two 50mm guns in casemates.

Still further west, Saint-Côme-de-Fresné is overlooked by the eastern flank of the plateau that surrounds Arromanches. Wn 39 was set into the plateau, facing eastwards and covering the whole of the coastal strip towards Ver-sur-Mer with two 75mm guns in casemates. On the plateau the Kriegsmarine had a radar station (**StP 42**) with a Seeriese FUMO 224 among other equipment. The coastal village of **Arromanches** was defended eastwards by Wn 43 with a casemated 75mm

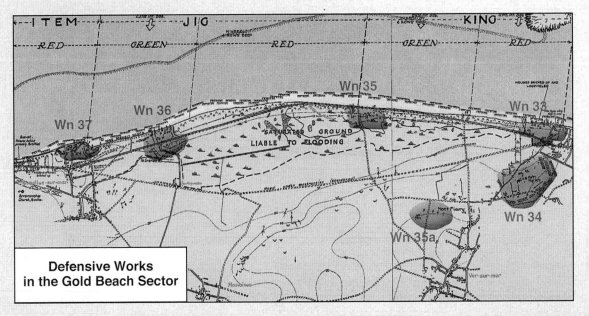

Wn 35

Wn 36

Wn 37

Wn 33

Wn 34

Wn 35a

SATURATED GROUND
LIABLE TO FLOODING

**Defensive Works
in the Gold Beach Sector**

The Landing

At 23.50 on June 5, RAF heavy bombers pounded the German artillery positions; 604 tons of bombs were dropped on the Longues battery and 585 tons on the battery at Mont Fleury. The sector was again attacked by U.S. 1st Bomb Division bombers at dawn on D-Day. At 05.10, the fleet opened fire on the coastal positions. At about 07.00, RAF fighter bombers attacked the Gold Beach defenses with bombs and rockets, and offshore LCTs fired thousands of rockets at the same targets.

At **07.25** 50th Infantry Division's **Force G** was off the five kilometers of beach at Gold Beach, King (from La Riviere to Hable de Heurtot), Jig (from Hable de Heurtot to Le Hamel), and Item, (from Le Hamel to Saint-Côme). 231st Infantry Brigade landed with two companies of 1st Hampshires on Jig Green, near Les Roquettes, with few casualties, and captured Wn 36 before proceeding west to **Le Hamel** (Wn 37). However this position was still intact despite the bombing, and hampered any further progress until two more companies arrived and assaulted the position again, this time with heavy

losses. By the evening of June 6, the 1st Hampshires had suffered 182 men killed and many more wounded (among them was the battalion commander, Lieutenant-Colonel N. Smith, who was wounded twice). It required the help of the Sherman tanks and self-propelled guns of the 147th Field Artillery Regt, and follow-up troops from the Devon and Dorset Regts to take the Le Hamel strongpoint at 16.00.

To the east, the 69th Infantry Brigade (6th Green Howards) came ashore at King Green at **07.25** to confront Wn 35 at Hable de Heurtot, manned by a company of Russian volunteers who put up only slight resistance. The Green Howards then got through the marshes over the narrow causeway to the Mont Fleury artillery battery. The shell-shocked Germans manning this battery surrendered without a fight.

Opposite La Riviere (Wn 33) on King Red, to the east of the sector, the 5th East Yorks met with stout German resistance from 7./736 and had to ask for support from the destroyers. Two special tanks were knocked out by the casemated 88mm

Sign on a lane up from the beach recalling the passage of 50th Infantry Division. (Photo, E. Groult/Heimdal).

VOIE DE LA
50ᵉ DIVISION D'INFANTERIE

50ᵉ INFANTRY DIVISION WAY

Gold Beach June 7, 1944. This flail tank belonging to C Squadron of the Westminster Dragoons (79th Arm'd Div.) was knocked out on the beach. In the background is the wreckage of an LCA and a DD tank of 4/7th Dragoons. (IWM).

gun, before being itself destroyed by three shells from a "Flail" tank. The strongpoint was captured at around 08.30 and 45 prisoners rounded up. Mopping-up operations continued until 10.00. Thirty prisoners were rounded up near Ver lighthouse. The 7th Green Howards landed at 08.20 and found no more Germans at Ver-sur-Mer although at the Mare Fontaine battery they captured fifty artillerymen from 6./1716 who had fired 87 rounds.

Coming in behind these two waves, reinforcements arrived at **07.30**. 1st Dorsets 231st Brigade landed near La Roquette and deployed westwards along the coast. C Company reinforced the position at Le Hamel and two other companies proceeded inland, reaching Meuvaines by 09.30.

The 2nd Devons landed at **08.15** opposite Le Hamel and were at once involved in heavy fighting. Two other companies had been landed too far to the east, at Les Roquettes, with the result that Jig Green beach was now badly overcrowded. Avoiding Le Hamel and Asnelles where 1st Hampshires were fighting, these two companies proceeded to Ryes where they were stopped by machine-gun and mortar fire. Ryes was not taken until 16.00. Other units of the two brigades landed in waves from 11.00 on.

Left: British cemetery at Bazenville: the grave of Major A.C.W. Martin of the Dorsetshire Regiment, killed on Gold Beach on June 6, 1944. (Photo, Georges Bernage/Heimdal).

Background photograph: the beach at Asnelles. (Erik Groult/Heimdal).

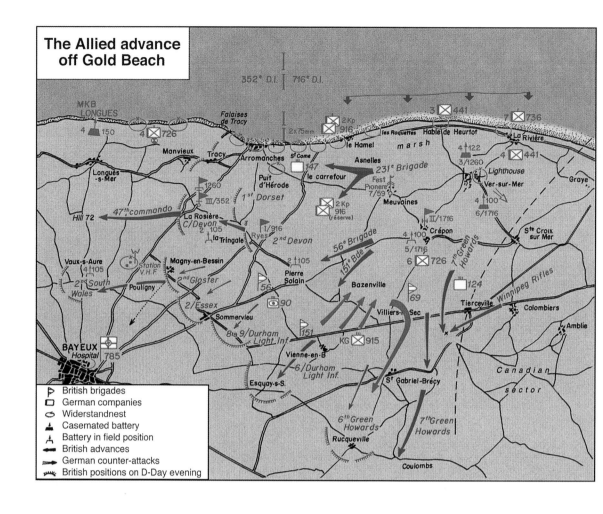

The Allied advance off Gold Beach

Map legend:
- British brigades
- German companies
- Widerstandnest
- Casemated battery
- Battery in field position
- British advances
- German counter-attacks
- British positions on D-Day evening

The advance inland

In the **west**, after reducing the Le Hamel strongpoint, the 1st Hampshires D Company advanced towards Arromanches, taking the coast road where they had the advantage of supporting naval firepower. They invested Arromanches at 21.00. After taking Meuvaines, the 1st Dorsets faced elements of IR 916's 1st Battalion near La Rosière just south of Arromanches, where it sustained a number of casualties. By the end of the day this battalion had lost 128 killed. From Ryes the 2nd Devons advanced towards La Rosière where they were pinned down, just south of the 1st Dorsets. By the end of day one the 2nd Devons had lost 80 men.

In the **south west**, 56th Infantry Brigade advanced towards Bayeux, 2nd Glosters reaching Magny-en-Bessin where they called it a day. The 2nd South Wales Borderers carried on advancing until 23.50, by which time they had reached Vaux-sur-Aure and seized the little bridge over the river; just a mile from Bayeux. Patrols with blackened faces from the 2nd Glosters even reached the N.E. outskirts of Bayeux (Saint-Vigor) at around 20.00, where they offered the young locals Navy Cut cigarettes and promised to be back at dawn. The 2nd Essexes settled for the night N.W. of Sommervieu, the spires of Bayeux cathedral seemed no distance away. At Saint-Martin-des-Entrées, 12 year-old Lecaudey spotted some British Bren carriers as early as 17.30.

In the **east**, advanced the 151st Brigade with three battalions of the Durham Light Infantry (DLI for short), the 8th and 9th DLI advancing to just south of Sommervieu whilst the 6th DLI got as far as Esquay-sur-Seulles.

In the **south**, 69th Infantry Brigade came up to Highway 13 and linked up with the Canadians. 6th Green Howards, who landed at Hable de Heurtot, held the line Esquay-sur-Seulles to Rucqueville that evening, very close to Highway 13.

At 16.00, ten assault guns of an anti-tank company of 352. ID counter-attacked at Crépon but were repulsed and what was left of the unit (6 assault guns and 90 men) fell back late in the day to Ducy-Sainte-Marguerite (south of Highway 13). 7th Green Howards took Creully, where they lost 4 tanks in crossing the River Seulles, moving on to Coulombs. Meanwhile this unit had linked up with the Canadian Winnipeg Rifles near Creully.

The Odyssey of 47th RMC

Formed in August 1943, the 47th Royal Marine Commando was under the command of Lieutenant-Colonel Phillips and attached to 231st Brigade for the landing operations.

The Marines landed at 08.30 on D-Day near Les Roquettes but unfortunately their fourteen landing craft were split up. At 08.50 the second-in-command, Major Donnell, mustered as many of 47th RMC as he could find, however 68 men and 4 officers including the CO were still missing. The unit's mission was to capture Port-en-Bessin as quickly as possible. Major Donnell and his men advanced westwards and reached Saint-Côme-de-Fresné where they linked up with the rest of the unit at 13.50. The whole party then moved on to La Rosière and Hill 72, south-east of Longues, and dug in for the night. Port-en-Bessin was still almost 4 1/2 km (3 mi) away!

Lieutenant-Colonel Philipps, commander of 47th RMC. His objective, Port-en-Bessin. (DR).

Outcome of the day

25,000 men came ashore in this sector, with 413 casualties on the beach and 89 landing craft lost. All objectives had been reached except in the west, where 47th RMC had failed to take Port-en-Bessin or link up with the Americans. But the troops were very near Bayeux.

June 6, 1944. elements of 50th Infantry Division (Green Howards) near Saint-Gabriel. (IWM).

Background photograph: Ver-sur-Mer, the road from Hable de Heurtot, defended by Wn 35. (Photo, Erik Groult/Heimdal).

1

2

Consolidation on June 7 & 8

1. British troops entered Bayeux on the morning of June 7, the first town to be liberated and captured intact. The town was used as a troop rest area. (IWM).

2. Aerial view of Port-en-Bessin in June 1944. The German strongpoints were set on the two plateaux overlooking the town to east and west. (IWM).

3. Port-en-Bessin with its vast harbor as it looks today from the old German strongpoint on the east side; a concrete emplacement can be seen in the foreground. (EG/Heimdal).

4. and 5. The first meeting of Allied commanders (the American Bradley and the Britishers Montgomery and Dempsey) took place at Port-en-Bessin on June 10, 1944. Here we see General Montgomery examining the port from his personnel vehicle. On the presentday photograph (5), the words "Bazar de Port-en-Bessin" are still inscribed on the house gable underneath "Ouistreham" added for the film "The Longest Day". (IWM and Heimdal).

Early on **June 7**, at 09.30, D.D Sherman tanks and other armored vehicles of 4/7th Dragoon Guards (8th Independent Armored Brigade) drove down the high street in **Bayeux** which thus became the first liberated French town. It was undamaged, and became a center for rest and relaxation for the troops. Five days later, General de Gaulle made his first speech from liberated France there.

To the west on June 7, 47th RMC advanced to **Port-en-Bessin** but found the Germans firmly entrenched there. After an attack by three squadrons of Typhoon fighter bombers, the commandos went up the main street and assaulted the German position overlooking the harbor to the west. They sustained about 40 losses to German machine-gunfire and flame throwers. This strongpoint finally fell but the other strongpoint on the plateau to the east also overlooking the harbor still held out, with the German garrison commander surrendering the following morning, **June 8** at 04.00 along with about fifteen men. Altogether, over the two days, 300 German prisoners were taken. Allied ships started using this harbor a few days later. A scene in the film "The Longest Day" depicting the assault on Ouistreham casino by commandos, was actually filmed in Port-en-Bessin, a "deliberate mistake" nevertheless based on fact.

On **June 8**, after the capture of Port-en-Bessin, 47th RMC linked up in the west with the GIs of 29th Infantry Division. This consolidation of the British and American sectors meant that the beachhead was now secure. In this sector the German front had ceased to exist and Major-General Graham commanding the 50th Infantry Division took charge of a tactical group consisting of the 151st Brigade and tanks of the 8th Independent Armored Brigade. His objective was the market town of Villers-Bocage, 22 km (14 mi) to the south! However a German armored division, the Panzer-Lehr-Division, had just arrived in the area and the two units met head-on near Ellon, marking the start of the battle of Tilly-sur-Seulles, which lasted until June 18!

6. and 7. That same day, French marines and Royal Navy marines began to use the outer harbor. Two days later five cargo ships were unloaded here. Later a pipeline was set up at Port-en-Bessin. (IWM and Heimdal).

8. and 9. Another view of the outer harbor. Here we see one of three German wrecks. (IWM and Heimdal).

3

4

6

5

7

9

8

1. The Gold Beach Museum at Ver-sur-Mer offers some interesting documents and objects relating to this sector. (EG/Heimdal).

2. Various buildings at Ver-sur-Mer recall the passage of the Allied troops. Here we see what was "Gold Inn", the residence of the staff officers of the Royal Navy 9th Beach Group who controlled all shipping in the Gold Beach sector as far as Arromanches. (EG/Heimdal).

3. Ver-sur-Mer, this villa housed Admiral Ramsay's HQ. (EG/Heimdal).

4. At Crépon, this bronze statue of a British soldier commemorates the action of 7th Brigade in the Gold sector. (GB/Heimdal).

5. The BBC's first radio station on French soil was set up in the keep of Creully Castle. General Montgomery set up his command post in the grounds of Château de Creullet just across the river. (EG/Heimdal).

6. Monument commemorating airfield B2 in front of Bazenville church. (GB/Heimdal).

7. The battery at Longues-sur-Mer is the only place on the Normandy coast where guns - 150mm guns - are still to be seen in their casemates. This exceptional site was used to film scenes for "The Longest Day". (EG/Heimdal).

8. Arromanches preserves vestiges of the artificial harbor, which is remarkably covered in the D-Day Landing Museum there. The all-round screen cinema on the cliff tops shows footage of the Battle of Normandy. (EG/Heimdal).

9. On June 14, 1944, General de Gaulle set foot once more on French soil, landing at Graye-sur-Mer. Here we see him emerging from the subprefecture building at Bayeux after making his first speech. (IWM).

10. The de Gaulle Museum in Bayeux, near the square where the general made his speech. (EG/Heimdal).

11. The Bayeux Battle of Normandy Memorial Museum offers an outstanding account of the military operations. (EG/Heimdal).

The British Sector after D-Day

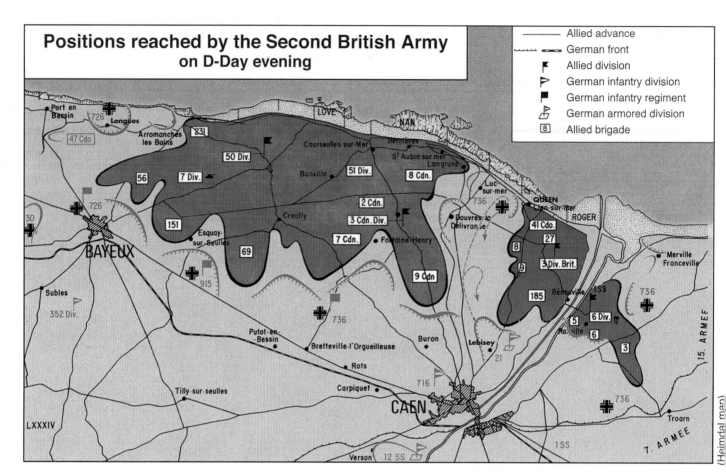

Positions reached by the Second British Army on D-Day evening

————	Allied advance
⌐⌐⌐⌐ ◼	German front
⌐	Allied division
▷	German infantry division
◼	German infantry regiment
◿	German armored division
8	Allied brigade

(Heimdal map)

A Canadian Churchill tank advancing through the Vaucelles southern neighborhood of Caen in July 1944. (PAC).

The objectives had only been achieved in part but by now the beachhead was firmly established. **In the west**, British troops were already in Bayeux on June 7. Two days later, heading towards Tilly-sur-Seulles, south of Bayeux, the 8th Armored Brigade Group came up against the leading elements of a crack division, the Panzer-Lehr-Division, arriving in reinforcement. A battle raged furiously for weeks in the "Bocage" or hedgerow country. **In the center,** 3rd Canadian Infantry Division was held in check on June 7 in an attempt to capture the airfield at Carpiquet west of Caen, when 12.SS-Panzer-Division, which had arrived in the sector the previous evening, launched a counter-attack against its flank; however, the German attack failed on **June 8 and 9** against Canadian troops now firmly entrenched in the villages on and near Highway 13 - Bretteville l'Orgueilleuse and Norrey-en-Bessin. Here too, a fierce battle lasted over a month. **To the east,** 3rd British Infantry Division was pinned down for a month before Caen. Further east, having received reinforcements, the airborne bridgehead was in a position to deal with any counterattacks. Then an initial offensive was launched on June 25 after being delayed by the storm; this was Operation Epsom, which was crowned with only limited success, reaching Hill 112 but failing to outflank Caen via the south. Finally, on **July 8**, the 3rd Canadian and 3rd British Infantry Divisions liberated Caen, by which time much of the city was in ruins. The major part of the German tank forces engaged in Normandy were concentrated in the Caen sector, which

Above: Cloth insignia of 21st Army Group HQ. This army group was in charge of all Allied ground forces engaged in Normandy, with General Bernard L. Montgomery in command. (Musée de Bayeux coll.).

Left: At 21st Army Group HQ at Creullet, early in June, from left to right: General Alanbrooke, Chief of the Imperial General Staff, Winston Churchill, General Bernard L. Montgomery. (IWM).

accounts for the ferocious fighting and limited results in this British sector, one month after D-Day. On **July 18**, a new offensive, Operation Goodwood, was launched east of the Orne River; the British tank forces sustained very heavy losses, but a week later, the front finally began to move as a breakthrough was made in the American sector (see pages 88 to 91).

Below: Lingèvres sector, June 15, 1944. Fearing a counter-attack by the Panzer-Lehr-Division, infantry of 50th Division dig a roadside trench. (IWM).

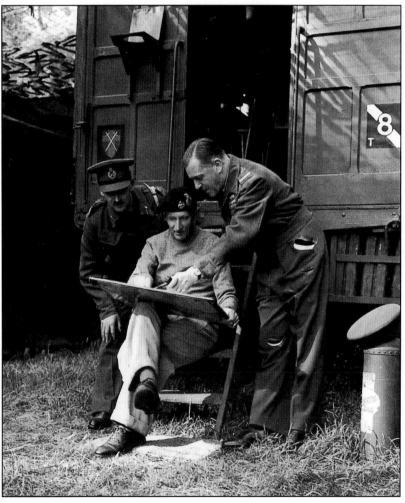

Above: In front of his caravan HQ, on which we see the 21st Army Group emblem, General Montgomery takes stock of the situation with his officers. His handling of the ground operations came in for some ferocious criticism in the American press. (IWM).

Omaha Beach

Cloth patch worn by the men of 1st Infantry Division, the famous "Big Red One". They also sometimes painted the emblem on their helmets. (Heimdal photo).

General Clarence R. Huebner (left), commander of 1st Infantry Division, reporting on the situation to Generals Eisenhower and Bradley. (US Army/ Heimdal coll.).

From Arromanches to Grandcamp, the Calvados coast is on high ground, with clay cliffs anything from thirty to sixty meters (100-200ft) high. Despite these difficulties, troops had to be brought ashore in the Omaha sector to enable British Second Army and American First Army to link up. There was one sandy beach about five kilometers (3mi) wide at the foot of the bluffs, which was where the landing would have to take place. This was Charlie, Dog, Easy and Fox on Omaha Beach. Such a difficult assignment was given to US V Corps (General Gerow) whose Force O was made up of 1st Infantry Division, 29th Infantry Division and the Rangers.

1st US Infantry Division
The Big Red One Division

The US Army's 1st Infantry Division was one of its most famous, having already performed with distinction during World War One and taken part in a number of operations prior to its D-Day preparations in England. Its insignia, a cloth shoulder flash, carries a "Big Red One" often stenciled on the men's helmets.

It was disbanded after the Great War, but reformed at Fort Benning, Georgia in November 1939. On November 8, 1942 it landed at Oran in Algeria during Operation Torch. There followed a hard battle first in Tunisia, then in Sicily before a return to England in October 1943. This was one of the few US divisions with plenty of battle experience, which is why it was assigned the difficult beach at Omaha, losing 1,744 men during the first week in Norman-

dy. The division was commanded by General Clarence Ralph Huebner (see box).

The division was made up of three Regiment Combat Teams or RCTs:

– 16th RCT had an infantry regiment (16th Infantry Regiment) reinforced by two artillery units (7th Field Artillery Battalion and 62nd Armored FAB), a tank battalion (741st Tank Battalion equipped with DD tanks) and engineers units.

– 18th RCT comprised 18th Infantry Regiment reinforced by two artillery units (32nd and 5th FAB), a tank battalion (745th Tank Battalion) and a few attached units.

– 26th RCT was made up of another infantry regiment (26th Infantry Regiment) reinforced by just one artillery unit (33rd FAB), a hospital company and a platoon of engineers. So it was the weakest of the three RCTs.

29th Infantry Division
The Blue and Gray Division

The US Army's 29th Infantry Division had taken part in the battles of the Meuse and the Argonne in 1918. It was a original division, built up from units of the National Guard, "citizen soldiers" recruited on the east coast of the United States, in Maryland, Virginia and Pennsylvania. It also had a rich historical tradition: when it was reformed, on February 3, 1941, its 115th Infantry Regiment was called "1st Maryland"; 116th Infantry Regiment was drawn from a Virginia Militia unit dating back to 1741; as for 175th Infantry Regiment, it was raised in 1774, when it was called the 5th Maryland. Its blue and

The commanding officer of 1st Infantry Division, **Clarence Ralph Huebner** was born on a Kansas ranch on November 24, 1888. He fought with distinction during the Great War, which he ended with the rank of Lieutenant Colonel. He took command of the Big Red One in August 1943 following the dismissal of Major General Terry de la Mesa Allen. In June 1944, at the age of 55, although in poor health (suffering terrible stomach pains) he prepared his division to perfection for its mission. He was a fine general, a stern disciplinarian who nevertheless had a great sense of humor and plenty of common sense. His tactical judgment was held to be infallible and his bravery under fire was described as "chivalrous". He took command of V Corps in January 1945. He was retired in November 1950, and died in 1972.

gray insignia – hence the division's nickname – recall the mixed origins of its men, from both northern and southern states, which had fought against each other during the American Civil War. Following intensive training in Cornwall, in SW England, this division was assigned to Omaha Beach and took Saint-Lô on July 18 following a fierce battle. By June 18, it had already sustained 3,500 casualties, about a thousand of them fatal. Its commander was General Charles H. Gerhardt (see box).

The German defenses

Between two sections of bluffs, the coastline drops over a distance of 5km (3mi) down to a vast sandy beach at the foot of a grassy plateau at a height of some forty meters (130ft). On this plateau stand three villages - respectively, from east to west, Colleville, Saint-Laurent and Vierville - with several small valleys linking the beach and the plateau. As the operations at Omaha Beach are extremely complex to follow, we shall describe the landscape and the German defenses for each American beach sector and inland village: Fox and Colleville sector, Easy sector and Saint-Laurent, Dog and Charlie sectors and Vierville. The sector was covered by fifteen German "resistance nests" (see map). The defending troops were elements of 352. Infanterie-Division (see chapter on "The Atlantic Wall"), but elements of 716. Infanterie-Division which had defended the sector until the arrival of 352. ID were also still in position, which meant that the troops defending Omaha Beach were more densely packed in Second British Army's eastern sector. Also three groups from an anti-aircraft corps (III. Flak-Korps) had been placed to the rear of the sector, behind Highway 13, armed with 36 fearsome 88mm guns. American veterans of 29th Division kept unhappy memories of the 88mm guns. And let's not forget the German 352nd Division's artillery guns. Its 1st Group was commanded by Major Pluskat, made famous by the film "The Longest Day", who had his command post at Château d'Etreham but who in real life was not at his Wn 60

The son of a career officer, General **Charles H. Gerhardt** was born in 1895. On leaving military college he fought in the Battle of St Mihiel and the Meuse and Argonne offensives in 1918. In 1942, Gerhardt was in Texas where he commanded 51st Cavalry Brigade. After commanding 91st Infantry Division, he took over 29th Infantry Division in July 1943. There he imposed his iron discipline on his citizen soldiers, breathing into them an offensive spirit. He it was who devised the division's war cry of "29th, Let's go!". He was extremely popular among the men, who called him Uncle Charlie. After the war he became a military attaché in Brazil. He died in Florida in 1976.

General Charles H. Gerhardt, commander of 29th Infantry Divison. (Heimdal).

observation post during the night of June 5 to 6, but with a lady friend in Bayeux! This regiment had 36 105mm guns and 12 150mm guns from Etreham to La Cambe.

Most of these defenses were set up between the winter of 1943 and the spring of 1944, at the instigation of Field Marshal Rommel. Several casemates in fact were not finished by D-Day. Had the Allies opted for Normandy instead of Italy for their landing in the summer of 1943, they would have met with only slight opposition…

Cloth patch worn by the men of 29th Infantry Division. (Heimdal).

Above. With its 50mm gun, this casemate belonging to Wn 65, where the Ruquet valley opens out, pinned down the first waves of landing troops, but after 10.00 American vehicles were able to move up the valley. (EG/Heimdal).

Left. To the far west of the sector, this casemate's aperture could enfilade the whole of Omaha Beach. At the time it housed a 75mm gun. Note the steep slopes at the top of the beach. (Heimdal photo).

1. Germans watching the beach from a range-finding post. (BA).

2. American RCT landing sectors at Omaha Beach. (Heimdal).

3. This is how US troops experienced the D-Day assault on Omaha Beach... (Heimdal coll.).

4. ... and this is how the war correspondents captured the moment for posterity. (NA/Heimdal).

Background photograph: Omaha Beach seen from where the American cemetery now stands, between what were strongpoints Wn 64 and (on the right) Wn 62. Wn 62 caused heavy losses among the landing troops. (G. Bernage/Heimdal photo).

"Bloody Omaha"

05.50, June 6. The destroyers of Force O opened fire on the coastline: USS Satterlee pounded the defenses at Pointe du Hoc. The Texas opened fire on the defenses of Dog sector, the Arkansas attacked the D3 exit, the Georges Leygues (of the Free French Naval Forces) and the Tanat Side took aim at E1 (on Easy), etc. But most of their shells fell a mile inland, killing a few cows.

06.00. The northwesterly wind had dropped, although still with gusts of up to 18 knots. The waves were three to six feet high. In the small assault craft, the men were weak with seasickness as they approached the coast. Then 480 B-24 bombers carrying 1,285 tons of bombs passed overhead. But owing to low cloud, the planes dropped their bombs too far inland. The mission was a total failure, with one bomb falling just behind Wn 62, and all the rest further back in the fields. The German positions remained intact whereas the troops coming ashore thought they had been wiped out ...

Opposite where the US cemetery now stands, the Sherman DD (amphibious) tanks of 741st Tank Battalion (116th RCT, 1st Div.) began to leave their twelve LCTs at 05.35. German shells soon started to rain on the LCTs. In heavy seas, only two DD tanks made it to the beach, the others foundered or their engines were flooded. When four tanks were brought directly onto the beach, after their LCT had been damaged by shellfire, opposite Vierville (Dog sector), Captain Elder and Lieutenant Rockwell decided, in view of the rough sea, to bring all 743rd Tank Battalion's DD tanks right up to the beach in their LCTs.

06.25. Squad 14 of the Special Engineer Task Force arrived off Easy Red opposite the Ruquet valley; the beach was deserted, they were early. Their LCM was hit by a shell, and they were all killed or wounded, the first Americans to die at Omaha Beach...

06.30. The leading wave arrived on the beach. The assault force was divided between the two divisions. To the east, 1st Infantry Division was committed with 116th RCT opposite Saint-Laurent and Colleville (Easy and Fox). To the west, 29th Infantry Division was committed with 16th RCT opposite Dog. However the undercurrents at Omaha Beach were very powerful at that time; on the rising tide, a side current runs all along the coastline in an eastward direction, reaching 2.7 knots 5 miles (8km) out to sea. The Rangers landing at Pointe du Hoc

(see chapter on "Pointe du Hoc") had to face the same problem but managed to reset their course in time. Off Omaha Beach, the early morning mist and smoke from the naval guns made it impossible to look for landmarks on the shore. The landing craft all drifted eastwards and the infantry came ashore opposite different targets from those for which they had been prepared. Nobody at all landed in some sectors, whilst elsewhere several companies were mixed up together as they came in at the same point. All this created a great deal of confusion further aggravated by the fierceness of the battle.

At Wn 62, opposite Fox Green, Captain Frerking was range-finding for the 105mm gun battery positioned at Houtteville. Beside him, Corporal Heinrich Severloh was firing an MG 42 machine-gun at a rate of 1,500 rounds a minute. It was 06.30. The artificial fog had lifted, revealing the Allied fleet 8 or 10 km (5-6mi) offshore. At Wn 62 there were eight artillerymen and eighteen infantrymen. Slightly to Frerking's left, Corporal Severloh saw American soldiers coming ashore just 800 meters away. He was preparing to follow the order issued by Captain Frerking: "When they are up to their knees in water, you must fire, and not until then!" So Severloh fired at the two columns of soldiers already in the water, coming down the side ramps of a troop transport vessel. The first man in each column fell, then the others behind him. More followed, and when they were up to their knees in water Severloh opened fire again. From Wn 62, on the right, Franz Gockel of 716th Infantry was also causing devastating losses to the assault troops with his Polish-built Bren gun. Also, again on Captain Frerking's instructions, radio operators Sossna and Gebauer sent orders to the artillery at the Houtteville battery (1./AR 352) and their shells exploded on the beach. Altogether by the end of his battle with the landing forces, Severloh had fired about 12,000 rounds with his MG 42 and 300 to 400 with his carbine.

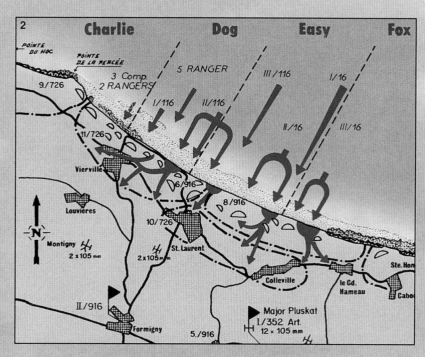

The Big Red One's ordeal

On Fox Beach opposite Colleville, 16th RCT E, F, I and L Companies hit the coast at 06.30, certain LCVPs arriving under what is now the US cemetery; the water was very deep and some of the men had to swim ashore, losing their heavy weapons. During the first hours of the assault, E Company registered 105 losses in this sector opposite beach exit E3. F Company was scattered and lost half of its men to machine-gun and mortar shell fire. And some of I and L Companies' landing craft drifted eastwards and landed too late.

In addition, most of 741st Tank Battalion's tanks capsized off Colleville, with just two making it ashore by 06.30 and able to offer support to the surviving Big Red One infantry. At 07.10, one of the two DD tanks knocked out one of Wn 61's 88mm guns.

A little to the west, on Easy Red, photographer Robert Capa also landed at 06.30: "… among the grotesque forms of the steel obstacles … a narrow strip of sand covered in smoke ; our Europe, Easy Red beach…". Here Robert Capa was to take the pictures remembered by posterity.

(Heimdal photo).

62

Above: photograph taken by Robert Capa.

(photos, NA/Heimdal coll.)

The Rangers' assault on the fortified house

To the west, at 06.20, 65 Rangers of 2nd Rangers Battalion were aboard two LCAs two hundred meters off Charlie beach. Not a shot was fired, but as soon as the ramps went down on the beach, a hail of machine-gun bullets and shells rained down on them. Most of the men in LCA 1038 were killed or wounded. A few minutes later the other LCA was smashed in two by three mortar shells and capsized. The survivors came to the foot of a 27m (90ft) cliff. Under Captain Goranson, they reached the top at around 07.30. At 07.00, an LCA of 116th RCT's B Company arrived in support. The Rangers captured the position known as the "fortified house" which had been a threat to Dog Beach.

07.00 - The second wave

The second wave did indeed reach Omaha Beach at 07.00. So far, the men were still pinned down on the beach, but the arrival of this second wave resolved the stalemate in several sectors. Apart from the Rangers who achieved their objectives (Wn 73 and Wn 72, far to the west), at 07.30, in the east, another success secured the capture of Wn 60.

16th RCT's L Company, which had drifted off course towards Port-en-Bessin, ended up landing at Fox Red (east of Colleville), in the shelter of the cliffs, at approximately 07.00. It moved to the foot of Wn 60 at 08.07, half an hour later the assault was launched, from both the side and rear. The strongpoint was captured at **09.00**, and 31 prisoners rounded up. After the left flank, the Germans' right flank had thus just collapsed.

Further elements were landed along the entire sector. At **07.10**, Major Bingham arrived before Wn 66 (Saint-Laurent) with 116th Regiment 2nd Battalion's command company. The assault was repulsed. 147th Engineer Battalion also came ashore. At **07.30**, General Norman Cota, Colonel Can-

ham and Major Howie landed between Wn 70 and Wn 68 (between Vierville and Saint-Laurent). This is where the major breakthrough was made.

On hearing the bad news of the troops pinned down on the beaches for over an hour with heavy losses, General Bradley planned on reembarking at 09.00 with a view to redeploying his troops at Utah and Gold Beach. Was the Omaha Beach landing to be a failure?

However, from 07.45 to 08.50, in 29th Division's sector, a number of local successes saved the day. At **08.30**, the first German prisoners were brought to an officer, they belonged to the 8th Company of 352nd Division's IR 916! The Americans had not catered for these reinforcements, the chiefs-of-staff had alone been informed two days previously, too late to warn the officers of the assault units.

At **09.30**, the breakthrough where now stands the American cemetery, between Wn 64 and Wn 62, was real enough but had been stopped in its tracks before the coast road and the village of Colleville by the firepower of German automatic weapons and mortar shells. However when General Bradley heard that his troops had broken through in several places, he dropped any thoughts of re-embarkation. Further inroads were made with some elements reaching the plateau between Wn 66 and Wn 65 at around 09.00, but they got bogged down and were unable to progress towards Saint-Laurent. Colonel Taylor had said on the beach: "two kinds of people are staying on this beach, the dead and those who are about to die. Now let's get the hell out of here!". Cota too broke through at around nine onto the flat ground between Wn 70 and Wn 68. To his left, elements of 5th Rangers Battalion were being machine-gunned by the Germans.

Among the elements that got through at the site where the US cemetery now stands was a platoon belonging to 16th RCT's E Company which attacked Wn 64 from the rear at 09.30. This position overlooked the Ruquet valley (beach exit E1). The

General Norman Cota, who directed the breakthrough on Dog White. (Heimdal coll.).

One of Robert Capa's famous photographs - soldiers sheltering behind beach obstacles. (NA/Heimdal).

position was captured at 10.00. Wn 65 covering beach exit E1 to the west was also attacked from the beach. This position's casemated 50mm gun was silenced at 10.30 and 20 prisoners were rounded up.

Exploiting the breakthrough, from 10.00 to noon

Wn 64 and 62 having fallen, the Engineers proceeded to clear beach exit E1. Troops and vehicles would begin to move up the Ruquet valley late in the morning. The last German coastal positions fell in turn.

Against Wn 62, the naval artillery fire was improving all the time; Heinrich Severloh was slightly wounded in the face and the aiming device was damaged. It had become impossible to hold the position and it was evacuated shortly afterwards as the Germans' final defenses collapsed under the naval shellfire.

And at D1, towards Vierville...

Faced with the strong position closing off D1, chiefly Wn 72 with a casemate housing an 88mm gun, a position further extended by a concrete chicane wall blocking the road, it took 14 hours for Sergeant N. Dube of 121st Engineer Battalion to place the demolition charges against the concrete wall, which was blown to pieces. The main access road inland to Vierville was opened at last early in the afternoon. Wn 72 was evacuated at 14.30. All German resistance had come to an end on the coast but during the afternoon Colleville was to remain in the hands of the Germans, of whom there were some 150 there at around 15.00. The church spire at Colleville was demolished by the naval guns and the village was completely surrounded by mid-afternoon.

Despite these successes, the Americans were slow to penetrate inland. The men were held up by pockets of resistance and by snipers. At 20.00, all vehicles were being directed to beach exits D1 (Vierville) and E1 (Le Ruquet), the only ones to have been properly cleared.

The outcome

34,250 men and 2,870 vehicles had already been brought ashore at Omaha Beach. The Germans had only about 2,000 men to oppose against them but the terrain was very much in their favor and the U.S. troops sustained heavy losses to avoid being thrown back into the sea and be able to penetrate inland. On the Allied side, total casualties among ground, naval and air forces rose to over 4,000 men for this sector on June 6, 1944. Losses by the evening of this decisive day were appalling indeed: 79 Sherman tanks were destroyed on the beach or capsized in the water. 29th Division had lost 2,440 men and 1st Division 1,744. 116th Regiment's H Company had been almost totally wiped out. 16th Regiment's E Company had lost 105 out of 180 men and the regiment as a whole registered 935 casualties. The preliminary bombing had been a failure since it had left the German positions intact, until the action by the Allied naval artillery, and most of all the bravery of a few individuals, averted total catastrophe. The Germans also suffered heavy losses, and with no reinforcements coming through, their last pockets of resistance gradually crumbled one after the other.

On June 7, mopping-up operations at Colleville were completed by around 10.00, and 52 dead Germans were found in the village. Towards noon, Highway 13 was crossed east of Formigny, a village that held out until evening. Progress was slow all day in all sectors. Grandcamp was not taken until June 8 once the Pointe du Hoc had been cleared.

More hard battles awaited 29th Infantry Division in the Saint-Lô sector. The terrible "battle of the hedgerows" was only just beginning. The American military cemetery at Colleville-sur-Mer is testimony to the great sacrifices made by the U.S. Army on Omaha Beach.

On Fox Red, to the east, a battlegroup leaves the shelter of the cliffs to join the front line. On the shingle lies various equipment including assault lifebelts. (NA/Heimdal coll.).

M1 US helmet, with the "Big Red One" emblem, and helmet liner on an assault lifebelt. (Heimdal photo).

1

2

MUSEE
OMAHA 6 JUIN 1944

3

MUSÉE

1. Remnants of Wn 62. This position put up some stout resistance until midmorning on D-Day, with losses to the landing troops. (GB/Heimdal).

2. The Musée Omaha 6 juin 1944 museum houses some interesting collections devoted to the Omaha Beach sector. (Heimdal).

3. D-Day Landing museum at Vierville-sur-Mer. (EG/Heimdal).

4. Monument to 1st Infantry Division near Wn 62, between the American cemetery and the beach at Colleville-sur-Mer. (GB/Heimdal).

5, 6. and background photo: various views of the American cemetery at Colleville-sur-Mer. (GB/Heimdal photos).

The Pointe du Hoc

The Rangers

During World War II, the US Army trained elite infantry battalions known as the Rangers. They were raised in order to carry out amphibious raids, assaults on strongpoints and missions requiring small units. They had to be capable of marching long distances. They were trained in hand-to-hand combat and in handling explosives.

The 1st Ranger Battalion was created on June 19, 1942 with 500 men selected from 2000 volunteers. It fought with distinction in North Africa. The 2nd and 5th Ranger Battalions were created on January 8, 1943 at Forest Camp, Tennessee.

On May 9, 1944, Lieutenant-Colonel James E. Rudder took over command of the Provisional Ranger Group comprising the 2nd and 5th Battalions. His assignment for Overlord was to storm the Pointe du Hoc. This was because the Germans had used this beauty spot overlooking the sea from the top of the sixty-foot cliff to set up a mighty artillery battery. Six concrete pits were built in 1942 to accommodate as many 155mm guns. It was one of the most powerful batteries in the whole Seine estuary, and it had the future Utah Beach sector within range. The position was reorganized on December 15, 1943. Stützpunkt Bayeux 075, as it was called, was occupied by 2./HKAR 1260 and, to protect the guns from aerial bombardment, three casemates were under construction, although only two of them were ready by D-Day, and the guns were lying in a sunken lane 200 meters south of the position awaiting installation. Lieutenant-Colonel Rudder was also assigned the task of landing some of his men at the western end of Omaha Beach to capture the Pointe de la Percée radar station and reinforce the assault units at the Pointe du Hoc. To do this, he divided his unit into two separate forces:

- Force A, with 2nd Ranger Battalion's D, E and F Companies, would launch the assault on the Pointe du Hoc at 06.30.

- Force C, with Lieutenant-Colonel Maxwell Schneider's 5th Ranger Battalion and 2nd Ranger Battalion's A and B Companies, was to be kept in reserve until it landed in turn at Dog Green (Omaha Beach). 2nd Battalion's C Company would be engaged near the Pointe de la Percée.

1. Helmet with the 2nd Ranger Battalion's emblem stenciled on the back. (Heimdal photo).

2. Lieutenant-Colonel James E. Rudder took command of the Provisional Ranger Group combining the 2nd and 5th Battalions and his major assignment was the assault on the Pointe du Hoc. This photograph was taken on June 8 after the mission had been successfully accomplished. (Heimdal coll.).

3. 9th US Air Force B-26 Marauders drop their heavy bombs on the German positions at the Pointe du Hoc. The Rangers can now launch their assault. (US Air Force).

4. Some of the Rangers in their LCVP prior to sailing for Normandy. (US Navy).

5. and 6. Cloth shoulder flashes worn by the men of the 2nd and 5th Ranger Battalions.

2nd Rangers at the Pointe du Hoc

1. The German range-finding post overlooking the Pointe du Hoc. (EG/Heimdal).

2. German flak emplacement east of the Pointe du Hoc. (EG/Heimdal).

3. The same spot in June 1944 as the Rangers lead away German prisoners after capturing the position. (US Army).

4. The Rangers set up a first aid post nearby. (US Army).

Background photograph: a gun emplacement devastated by the bombing. (EG/Heimdal).

05.45. The men of 2nd Ranger Battalion had left the two Liberty Ships, HMS Ben Machreet and HMS Amsterdam, to board 12 small LCAs and 4 DUKWs, but they were still 12 nautical miles (20km) off the coast in their tiny landing craft when already one of them, LCA 914, was overturned by a huge wave and capsized, leaving only one survivor, Pfc John Riley of D Company.

Colonel Rudder's 225 Rangers had already had a rough time of it, having embarked on June 2, enduring a storm while down in the Liberty Ships' holds, they were ill and exhausted even before sailing during the night of June 5-6.

The coast was still too far off to see. A second landing craft, LCA 860, capsized but the 20 men and Captain Slater got out in time. These were dangerous seas for flat-bottomed barges, and afraid they might sink, the Rangers baled out water with their helmets. They were three miles off the coast when Sergeant Lomell noticed they had drifted about 5km (3mi) eastwards, off the Pointe de la Percée. He reported it to Colonel Rudder (LCA 888) who told them to get back on course, but then a German 20mm gun at the Pointe de la Percée opened fire, hitting a DUKW and killing or wounding five of the nine Rangers in it. The LCs had to move along the cliffs to reach their objective.

06.30. The British destroyer Talybont, which had opened fire on the Pointe du Hoc, stopped firing, this being H Hour for the Rangers, who were late owing to the navigational error. This left the Germans 30 minutes to recover after the heavy shelling they had just received and filter back to their combat stations to greet the Rangers with their small arms.

The 9 remaining LCAs of the assault force then turned to face the cliffs and come in slightly to the east of the Pointe du Hoc. The time was **07.10.** The first Rangers jumped out of their LCs onto a shingle beach at the foot of the cliff, 40 minutes late. The nine landing craft came ashore on a 450m (1500ft) wide front. The Rangers came under machine-gun fire from the left while USS Satterlee shelled the Pointe du Hoc. LCA 888 was first to land carrying Lieutenant Colonel Rudder, his radio operator and members of the support company. Spotting some German soldiers on the cliff top, Sergeant Domenick B. Boggetto opened fire. One of them was hit and fell to the ground, the rest disappeared.

In front of LCA 888, the bombs had caused a landslip, with part of the cliff reduced to a 12m (40ft) high pile of rubble, which helped to scale the cliff with a 5m (16ft) fireman's ladder. T5 George J. Putzek was first to reach the top, where he was badly wounded. Other Rangers hooked their grappling irons onto the cliff top and climbed up ropes dangling down from them.

Within fifteen minutes, all the men of D Company from LCA 888 had reached the cliff top. On the far right, LCA 861 with Lieutenant Theodore E. Lapres and his men of E Company came aground on the shingly beach, followed by LCA 862 carrying fifteen

men, also of E company. Twenty yards to the left of Lieutenant-Colonel Rudder's LCA 888, LCA 772 came ashore with another fifteen Rangers of that company. Only two of their grappling irons reached the cliff. E company landed on the right, with D company in the center and F company on the left.

On the cliff top, the companies organized themselves amid a lunar landscape with huge bomb craters everywhere. The real battle was only just beginning as they made their way forward from crater to crater under German gunfire. The concrete range-finding post was destroyed by tossing three grenades and firing a bazooka through the lookout slit. The Rangers passed by the empty casemates before heading off south to discover the guns which had been removed from the position by the Germans. About fifty Rangers moved along the road. Sergeant Lommel had noticed thick caterpillar trackmarks leading to the sunken lane where the Germans had concealed the guns in firing position, south of the tarmacked road which they reached at around **08.00.** Towards 09.00, Sergeants Lommel and Kuhn discovered five 155mm GPF guns. Lommell placed thermite grenades against the training mechanism and breech-block, rendering the five guns useless.

But the Germans surrounded this forward position and even brought in reinforcements from Grandcamp, leaving the Rangers to fight elements of 11./914 and 9./726. By now the Rangers were spread out and had to fight a fierce battle to fend off this German counterattack. Some fifty of them held a defensive line south of the road, while the others resisted amid the chaos of the stricken battery emplacement. Reinforcements did not arrive until next morning and the men were only rescued on June 8, down to 120 unwounded, with 77 killed.

Lt-Col. Rudder had good reason to be worried. His forces had to land on a narrow beach, scale a sheer six-storey high cliff and destroy the German battery. Admiral Hall's intelligence officer remarked, it can't be done. Three old women with brooms could stop the Rangers scaling that cliff. When Rudder realized just how important the mission was, he just told General Bradley, Sir, my Rangers can do the job for you.

Les Rangers, l'assaut de la Pointe du Hoc, by R. Lane, Editions Heimdal.

Bibliography:

- Rudder's Rangers, by Lieutenant-Colonel Lane, Manassas 1979, a detailed account of the battle.

4

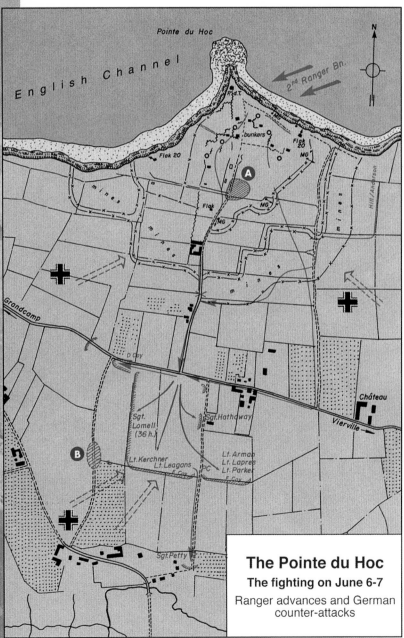

The Pointe du Hoc

The fighting on June 6-7

Ranger advances and German counter-attacks

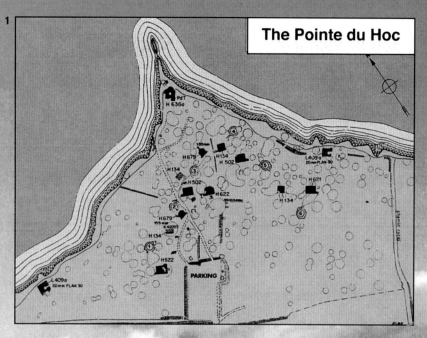

The Pointe du Hoc

1. The Pointe du Hoc, site plan. (Heimdal).

2. The 155mm guns that were supposed to equip the casemates of the Pointe du Hoc battery were located in a sunken lane south of the coast road. One of them is shown in this American photograph taken just after the battle. (NA/Heimdal).

3. One of the casemates of the Pointe du Hoc battery. (EG/Heimdal).

4. and background photograph. Concrete gun emplacements smashed to pieces by heavy bombs. (EG/Heimdal).

5. Along Highway 13, the German military cemetery at La Cambe, containing the graves of 21,222 German soldiers, is one of the biggest in Normandy. (EG/Heimdal).

6. Grandcamp. The monument to the French heavy squadrons that fought alongside the RAF. (EG/Heimdal).

7. Grandcamp. The interesting Ranger Museum. (EG/Heimdal).

8. Grandcamp. The monument to the US National Guard. (EG/Heimdal).

Musée des Rangers, 30, Quai Crampon, 14450 Grandcamp-Maisy. Tel. +33 (0)231 923351.

Open daily from April 1 to October 30, from 10.00 to 19.00, Monday from 13.00 to 19.00

Utah Beach
Sainte-Marie-du-Mont

The Cotentin peninsula protrudes into the sea with all of its northern part fringed by a rocky coast with plateaus culminating at 178m (585ft). The south-eastern area between Valognes (north) and Carentan (south) drops down to the sea to form a plain called, unsurprisingly, "Le Plain". This great plain extending from north to south is surrounded by marshlands, to the west by the Merderet marshes, to the south by the Douve marshes, and to the east, between the coastal plain and the dunes. Normally speaking, these well-drained marshlands are dry for most of the year and flooded in winter. Seeing their defensive potential, the Germans inundated them permanently using a system of locks and floodgates.

This low-lying coastline, codenamed Utah Beach, was chosen to land the US VII Corps. From this beach, assault divisions landing on the beach would have to consolidate a lodgment area, seal off the Cotentin to the west, then advance northwards to capture the rest of the peninsula, notably the major port of Cherbourg through which to land the additional supplies needed to pursue the offensive. But to ensure a successful landing the bridges over the flooded areas had to be seized both to help the incoming troops penetrate inland and to control bridges to the south and west in the flooded areas for purposes of breaking out of the beachhead.

Two airborne divisions - 82nd Airborne and 101st Airborne - were assigned to this operation. 101st Airborne was given the southern section of the Cotentin beachhead and was to be dropped near Sainte-Marie-du-Mont. It would then link up with 4th Infantry Division landing at Utah Beach and later with 9th Infantry Division (on D+4) and 79th Infantry Division (on D+8). US VII Corps would then be at full strength.

The German defenses

From Saint-Vaast-la-Hougue to Baie des Veys (Carentan), the beach defenses fell to Grenadier-Regiment 919 under the command of Oberstleutnant Günter Keil (command post on Hill 69, west of Quinéville). An experienced officer, Lt-Col Keil had under his command soldiers who were no longer young, as 75% of his NCOs and men were between 35 and 45 years old. Most of them had only had eight weeks military training, whilst a mere 25% were veterans from the Russian front. A vast 35km (22mi) sector was to be covered. The regiment held the first 25 strongpoints of the eastern

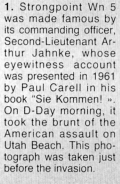

1. Strongpoint Wn 5 was made famous by its commanding officer, Second-Lieutenant Arthur Jahnke, whose eyewitness account was presented in 1961 by Paul Carell in his book "Sie Kommen! ». On D-Day morning, it took the brunt of the American assault on Utah Beach. This photograph was taken just before the invasion.

2. Jahnke's men strengthen the position. (ECPA).

coast of the Cotentin, from Le Grand Vey (Wn 1 = lightly fortified strongpoint) to Aumeville-Lestre (Wn 25). Four of them, StP 9, 12, 16 and 18 were heavily fortified strongpoints, or Stützpunkte.

The beach zone opposite the future American landing zone was held by the regiment's 1st Battalion (1./919), under Captain Fink. South of the sector, two companies were turned towards the Baie de Veys: 1./919, commander Lieutenant Gluba, and 2./919 under Second Lieutenant Rohweder (wounded on June 7). Facing east, the strongpoints were held by 3./919 under the command of Lieutenant Malz (killed on June 6), then by 4./919, commander Lieutenant Werner. The landing would take place against this company. It was planned opposite Wn 8 and StP 9. It actually took place opposite Wn 5 commanded by Second Lieutenant Arthur Jahnke, a brilliant officer who had been awarded the Bar for Close Combat and a Knight's Cross in the Order of the Iron Cross. The position was lightly armed (four 60mm guns, one 47mm gun and one 37mm gun). Further north, strongpoint StP 9 was better armed with two casemated 88mm guns and 5 tank turrets with 37mm guns. These coastal positions set in the dunes were isolated from the hinterland by opening

sluice gates and flooding the low marshy areas, leaving only a few through roads.

A battalion commanded by Captain Stiller was held in reserve to the rear near Turqueville - Georgisches Battalion 795 made up of Georgian volunteers, former Soviet citizens hailing from the Caucasus. Also, an artillery group 1./1261 (command post at Foucarville near 1.919's) covered the sector with its firepower, particularly from its casemated French 105mm Schneider guns of the Azeville Battery (2./1261). Another battery was set up at Saint-Martin-de-Varreville with four 122mm Russian-built guns, positioned near the tiny village of La Croix aux Berlots. The third battery (3./1961) was more dangerous, being equipped with four Czech 210mm Skoda guns (with a range of 27km/17mi) and one 150mm gun. Two of the 210mm guns were housed in thick concrete casemates. This battery was actually a naval artillery unit attached to the regiment. Its commander was Oberleutnant zur See Walter Ohmsen.

The shoreline defenses were not very powerful and the Georgian battalion was a poor quality reserve force. But the American assault force still had to get across the inundated area under direct threat from three artillery batteries.

3. Plan of strongpoint Wn 5 which took the brunt of the American assault on Utah Beach. (Map, B.Paich/Heimdal).

4. On this color photograph taken from a concrete type H677 casemate after the landing, the 8.8cm Pak gun continues to cover the length of the dune-topped beach at Varreville (Stp 9). Allied blockships scuttled as breakwaters can still be seen. (A.Chazette/Heimdal coll.).

The Airborne Operation during the night of June 5-6

101st Airborne

This great unit was re-formed on August 16, 1941 under the command of Brigadier General William C. Lee who came to be known as the "father of the American airborne army". This unit was heir to the Iron Brigade which wore an "Old Abe" eagle's head during the American Civil War. The new unit took up this eagle's head on the paratroopers' shoulder flash, hence the nickname "Screaming Eagles". The division comprised four infantry regiments of three battalions each.

- 501st Parachute Infantry Regiment was commanded by Colonel Howard Johnson, 502nd P.I.R. by Colonel George Moseley, and 506th P.I.R. by Colonel Robert Sink. A fourth regiment - 327th Glider Infantry Regiment - was to be brought over by gliders (its 1st Battalion was replaced by the 1st Battalion of 401st G.I.R.). Unlike 82nd Airborne Division, which had already been engaged in Sicily, 101st Airborne Division lacked any such experience. Colonel Johnson, the energetic and demanding commander of 501st Regiment, was determined to turn his men into crack troops. L. Critchell in Four Stars of Hell tells how Johnson wanted killers; he wanted to meet force with even greater force; he wanted a regiment that could be molded into a single weapon. He would accept no human weakness. After General Lee suffered a heart attack, General Maxwell D. Taylor took over command of the division in March 1944, having previously been chief-of-staff with 82nd Airborne. His second-in-command was Brigadier General Don F. Pratt.

The division was tasked to secure the exits of the four roads from the coast, capture Sainte-Marie-du-Mont which was on a crossroad, destroy the Saint-Germain-de-Varreville gun battery, destroy and seize the bridges north of Carentan, including the floodgate of La Barquette, reach Highway 13 at a place called Les Forges, link up with 82nd Airborne Division and secure the Douve Valley north-west of Carentan.

The operations

At **21.50** on June 5, 11 C-47s took off from Great Britain carrying pathfinders to mark out the objectives. These pathfinders, led by Captain Frank L. Lillyman, would be the first Allied soldiers to set foot on Norman soil. They were dropped at **00.16.** Drop Zone A (DZ A) in the north was set up for 502nd P.I.R., south-west of Saint-Martin-de-Varreville (near the German gun battery). In the center, DZ C was set up for 506th P.I.R. west of Sainte-Marie-du-Mont. DZ D was to be set up in the south for 501st P.I.R. between Vierville and the La Barquette lock. But, owing to a navigational error, the pathfinders heading for this last DZ were dropped a kilometer (2/3 mile) away from their objective.

Half an hour later, it was the paratroops of 101st Airborne's turn for the airdrop in Operation Albany. This mobilized a huge fleet of 432 C-47s carrying 6,789 paratroopers. The first men, belonging to 1/506, were dropped at **01.14;** half of the sticks landed in their DZ, the rest were scattered. 2/506 was scattered over a wide area with some paratroopers jumping over Sainte-Mère-Eglise. On the whole, the men were dispersed with the loss of 36 aircraft.

Securing the beach exits

This mission was carried out by elements of 502nd and 506th P.I.R. But after sunrise:

- From **DZ A**, after catastrophic jumps, 2/502 and Lieutenant Colonel Chappuis captured the (destroyed) Saint-Martin-de-Varreville battery. Lieutenant Colonel Cassidy (1/502) with Captain Lillyman reached Foucarville where they held the northern front of the parachute sector. Lieutenant Colonel Cole (3/502), was dropped too far to the west and lost a lot of time looking for his way before reaching

1. General Maxwell D. Taylor, commander of 101st Airborne Division (US Army/Heimdal).

2. These US paratroopers aboard a C-47 are about to be dropped over the Cotentin peninsula. (NA/Heimdal).

3. American helmet with stenciled on it an ace of clubs, the emblem of 327th Glider Infantry Regiment. The paratroopers of 501st PIR had an ace of diamonds on their helmets. (Heimdal photo).

4. Brigadier General Don Pratt was killed when his glider landed at 04.08 on June 6, 1944. (Heimdal coll.).

5. Damaged Waco glider. (NA/Heimdal).

6. Cloth arm patch worn by the men of 101st Airborne Division. (Heimdal photo).

7. (Background photograph): gliders landing on D-Day. (NA/Heimdal).

Exit 3 at 07.30. Captain Clemens reached Exit 4 a little further north.

- From **DZ C** a group of about 145 paratroops led by two generals (Taylor and Mc Auliffe) and Lieutenant Colonel Ewell (CO of 3/501, attached to 506th P.I.R.) reached Pouppeville (opposite Exit 1) at around 08.45, facing Germans they had to fight all morning on D-Day. 18 paratroops were killed. Taylor said, "Never have so few been commanded by so many (officers)." Sainte-Marie-du-Mont was captured by paratroops landing in this Drop Zone. In this sector, Lieutenant Colonel Strayer managed to assemble some 400 men (mostly from 2/506) on their way to Houdienville at **04.30.** But at around 09.30 Strayer was pinned down by 13./919's 76.2mm guns before reaching Exit 2, and had to wait until 8th RCT arrived with its tanks.

Attacking west and southwards

DZ D received the paratroops of Colonel Johnson's 501st P.I.R., at least Lieutenant Colonel Robert A. Ballard's 1st Battalion, which came down south of Angoville and attacked due west. Major Allen (2/501) also attacked due west towards Basse-Addeville. To the south, Colonel Johnson marched towards La Barquette with 150 men to seize the bridge across the Douve. The lock was soon captured and positions organized on the south bank. 3/506 landed at 01.43 in the center of the DZ straight into the waiting Germans' hands. Lieutenant Colonel Wolverton, commander of 3/506, was killed almost at once, and many of his men were mown down by mortar and machine-gun fire. This sector was where German counterattacks from the south, including by von der Heydte's paratroops, had to be contained.

The death of General Pratt

A little before dawn, two gliders arrived over **LZ E.** One, piloted by Lieutenant Colonel Mike Murphy, was the Fighting Falcon bringing 101st Airborne Division's second-in-command, Brigadier General Don Pratt. The other brought part of 326th Medical Company. But there was a very strong side-wind and Mike Murphy landed in a meadow bathed in a very heavy morning dew. The gliders started to aquaplane, crashing into a hedgerow 250m (800ft) from the D 329 road (SW of Hiesville). General Pratt and Lieutenant Buttler were both killed instantly. The time was **04.08.**

The Utah Beach landing

4th US Infantry Division
The "Ivy" Division

The US Army's 4th Infantry Division was established in 1940. Its chief-of-staff, Raymond O. Barton, took over command in June 1942. It followed a rugged training course with amphibious exercises at Camp Gordon, Florida, before being transferred to the UK in January 1944, where it took part in more amphibious exercises at Slapton Sands. Although it had no battle experience, it was "superbly trained".

It comprised three infantry regiments:
- 8th Infantry Regiment, commander Colonel James A. Van Fleet;
- 12th Infantry Regiment, commander Colonel Russel P. Reeder;
- 22nd Infantry Regiment, commander Colonel Hervery A. Tribolet;
- with reinforcement from four artillery battalions, 20th Field Artillery Battalion, 29th FAB, 42nd FAB and 44th FAB.

It was placed under the command of General Raymond C. Barton. Born in 1889, he graduated from the American Military Academy in 1912. As early as August 1919, he was sent to France to join the 8th Infantry Regiment, taking over its command at the end of 1938. In 1940, he became chief-of-staff of the division to which 8th I.R. was attached. Barton was a good instructor and his men received in-depth training. He died at Fort Gordon, Georgia, on February 27, 1963.

The landing

At **04.30**, four men armed only with knives swam up to the creeks of the Saint Marcouf islands, a tiny archipelago whose two main islands stood immediately opposite the planned landing zone. There were no Germans there.

A quarter of an hour after this first capture, at **05.45,** the invasion fleet was approaching the coast. The warships of Task Force 125 then opened fire to knock out the German defenses. USS Nevada's target was the Azeville battery, while Erebus took aim at La Pernelle, Tuscaloosa and Quincy Mont Coquerel and Saint-Marcouf/Crisbecq, Hawking Saint-Martin-de-Varreville (already destroyed by aerial bombardment), Black Prince engaged Morsalines and Enterprise the landing zone. The sloop Soemba concentrated its attack on the beach defenses. A few minutes later, 276 Marauders of the 9th US Air Force dropped 4,404 tons of bombs on seven targets from Wn 3 to Wn 10 with devastating results. The strongpoints were very badly hit and all telephone connections between German strongpoints were cut off. Lieutenant Colonel Keil could no longer give orders beyond his command post and so was unable to organize a

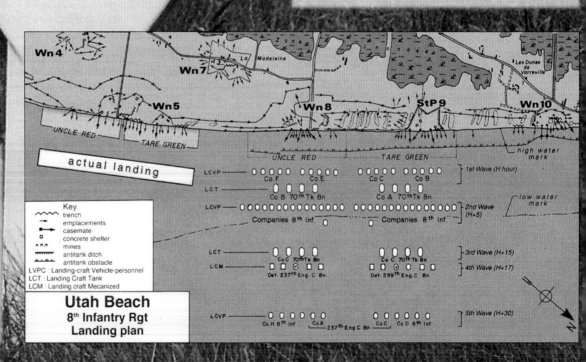

1. Cloth badge of VII Corps.

2. Cloth badge of 4th Infantry Division. (Heimdal photos).

3. US soldiers near the "Chalet Rouge" in Wn 5. (NA/Heimdal). We see in the background photograph the same house as it is today and a signpost in honor of Private Calandrella. (EG/Heimdal).

Brigadier General Theodore Roosevelt

The son of President Theodore Roosevelt, he was born in 1887. He was a frail, poor-sighted young man who nevertheless fought with great courage with 1st Infantry Division during World War I. He later wrote books and entered politics. He joined the army again in 1941, and saw action in north Africa and Sicily. He insisted on joining the first assault waves armed with no more than his .45 colt and walking-stick... He landed in Corsica, then joined 4th Infantry Division, persuading General Barton to let him land with the first wave in Normandy. His considerable experience and bravery ensured success at Utah Beach and earned him a Medal of Honor. On July 12, 1944, having been promised command of 90th Infantry Division, he faced a counter-attack by 17. SS-Panzergrenadier-Division "Götz von Berlichingen" near Carentan. So intense was the battle that he died of a heart attack in a school playground at Méautis, at the age of 57. He was buried at the US cemetery at Colleville-sur-Mer in "D" square facing out to sea. Another Roosevelt is buried alongside him - his brother, a pilot killed during the Great War and who was brought here for them to lie side by side.

coordinated defense. Cut off from each other, the survivors had to fend for themselves.

However, the landing fleet failed to arrive at its planned destination. In the unusual currents along the eastern coast of the Cotentin, producing a kind of "alternative tide", the ships had drifted off course to the south on the rising tide, with a stronger and shorter current. Instead of facing Wn 8 and StP 9, they were within sight of Lieutenant Jahnke's Wn 5, or what was left of it. But this navigational error turned out to be a blessing in disguise as the landing took place 2.5km (1.5mi) further south in a less exposed area almost out of range of the Saint Marcouf and Azeville batteries.

From **06.20 to 06.40**, P-47 Thunderbolts carried out a rocket attack on the shore batteries to finish the job of silencing them. At **06.40**, twenty LCVPs brought in the first wave of 8th RCT, F and E Companies to the left at Uncle Red, and C and B Companies to the right, at Tare Green ten minutes later. About 300m (330yds) from the beach, the company commanders fired special smoke projectiles to request the ships to lengthen their range. Brigadier General Theodore Roosevelt came ashore at Uncle Red with the first wave. 70th Tank Battalion followed closely behind with its DD tanks. In view of the navigational error, General Roosevelt dispatched a recce party inland after Wn 5 had been taken rather easily. He located the causeway leading inland, Exit 2 towards Sainte-Marie-du-Mont. As things were going pretty well, the decision to press on in this sector was upheld.

The 237th Engineer Battalion cleared the beach and made breaches in the antitank wall. Within an hour the way was clear. At **08.00** Colonel Van Fleet's 8th Infantry Regiment and 3rd Battalion, 22nd Infantry Regiment had all come ashore. The rest of 22nd Infantry had landed by 10.00 as 8th Infantry Regiment advanced inland. Its 1st Battalion moved forward to the right towards La Madeleine and Wn 7, and further north to Exit 3 on its way to Audouville-la-Hubert. The Germans were demoralized and did not put up much of a fight. In the cen-

ter, the next battalion (3/8) proceeded to Exit 2, heading for Sainte-Marie-du-Mont. Meanwhile 2/8 turned south to Wn 2 (La Petite Dune) before veering westwards via the short causeway leading to Exit 1, and on to Pouppeville, arriving at 12.00.

---

4. Brigadier General Theodore Roosevelt Jr.

5. Major General Raymond O. Barton, commander of 4th Infantry Division.

6. June 1944, 6th: Aerial view of the American troops on Utah Beach.

(NA/Heimdal).

1. Infantrymen, having come off the beach still wearing their lifebelts advance along a road in 10cm (4in) of water in the inundated area as they penetrate inland. (DAVA/Heimdal coll.).

Linking up with the paratroopers

At noon, the 4th Division's 3rd Infantry Regiment, 12th RCT, landed in its turn. Meanwhile, the three battalions pressed relentlessly on inland in the face of the German 1st Battery, 352nd Artillery Regiment which opened fire on Utah Beach. Further north, 1/8 reinforced by A Company of 70th Tank Battalion reached Exit 3 already held by Lieutenant Colonel Cole's paratroops (3/502), and then proceeded beyond Audouville-la-Hubert, to be stopped approaching Turqueville at nightfall by Captain Stiller's Georgian battalion. In the center, 3/8 reached n° 2 Exit after losing 2 DD tanks. At La Vienville, a little beyond the Exit, they destroyed 3 or 4 of 13./919's Russian-built 76.2mm guns. They linked up with Lieutenant Colonel Strayer's paratroops (2/506). 3/8 reached Les Forges on Highway 13 late in the day. Task Force Howell, whose mission was to link up with 82nd Airborne, took the same route, only to be pinned down at Les Forges and so was unable to join 82nd at Sainte-Mère-Eglise. Further south, 2/8 passed through Pouppeville and linked up with Taylor's 3/501 before moving on through Sainte-Marie-du-Mont, also reaching Les Forges on Highway 13.

D-Day results

In this sector, VII Corps achieved its major objectives. The landing was a success and casualties moderate, with 4th Division losing 197 men including 60 missing. Out of this total the two principal regiments engaged, 8th and 22nd, took only 118 losses, 12 fatal. And huge quantities of equipment were brought in behind the assault troops. 101st Airborne Division's losses were much heavier in this sector, particularly when gliders brought in reinforcements later in the day. Many of them crashed on LZ E (west of Hiesville) when they came under German fire after **20.00.** 258 men were killed or wounded on Hill 30. Apart from that, whilst the beachhead had been firmly established between Sainte-Marie-du-Mont and the sea, further west the Americans paratroops were still in isolated groups surrounded by Germans and the assault troops had not yet linked up with Sainte-Mère-Eglise. Lastly, German paratroops of von der Heydte's 6th Regiment had launched a counterattack in the south, encountering 501st PIR at Basse-Addeville, and after capturing the positions there had reached Vierville late in the afternoon.

Another photograph by war correspondent Kaye showing a group of paratroopers of 101st Airborne in front of the pump opposite the church at Sainte-Marie-du-Mont. The civilian population is amazed and delighted to see these soldiers dropping out of the sky... (DAVA/Heimdal coll.).

The same spot as it is today. (Heimdal).

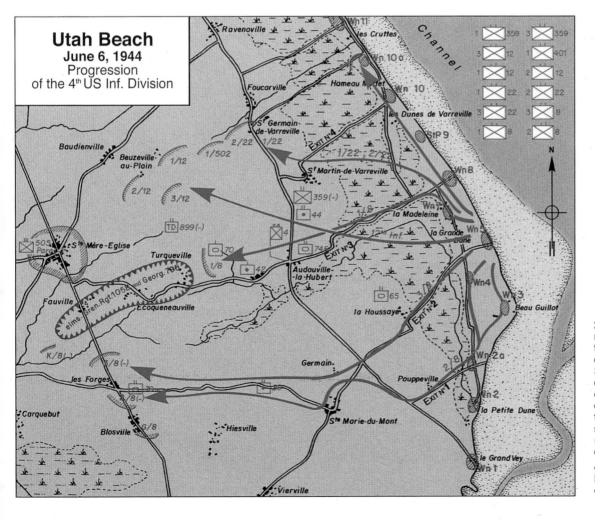

Utah Beach
June 6, 1944
Progression
of the 4th US Inf. Division

2. and 3. US war correspondent Kaye took these two photographs of the main square at Sainte-Marie-du-Mont, dominated by the church as paratroopers of 101st Airborne pass through. Note the Weasel tracked vehicle. (Photos, DAVA/Heimdal coll.).

4.and 5. Today, nothing has changed... (Heimdal photos).

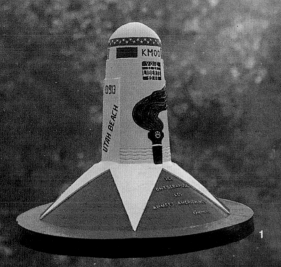

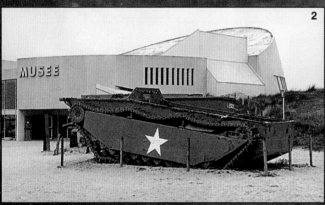

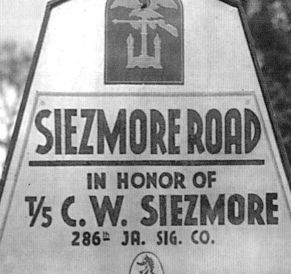

SIEZMORE ROAD
IN HONOR OF
T/5 C. W. SIEZMORE
286th JA. SIG. CO.
KILLED IN ACTION   JUNE 15th 1944

1. On the site of Wn 5 at Utah Beach, next to the museum, stands the "Kilometer 00" milepost, marking the starting point of what is known as 4th Infantry Division's Liberty Highway across France and Holland as far as the German border. There is one every kilometer from Utah Beach to Sainte-Mère-Eglise. (Heimdal).

2. and 3. The Musée du Débarquement at Utah Beach was built on the historic site of Wn 5, amid the concrete casemates in what remains of this German position. This interesting D-Day museum is surrounded by American equipment used at the time. (Heimdal photos).

6 JUIN 1944

4. The Leclerc Monument: General Patton's Third Army and General Leclerc's French 2nd Armored Division landed a little way north of where the Utah Beach museum now stands, across the dunes at Varreville. The French D-Day Committee has erected a "signal monument" to commemorate that event. An M8 armored car and a half-track in the colors of 2nd Armored are also sited here. (Heimdal).

5. The naval battery at Crisbecq (Saint-Marcouf) (3./HKAR 1261) continued firing its 210mm guns on the northern sector of Utah Beach until June 11, 1944. Here we see one of the enormous type H 683 casemates blown open after the battle when the Americans carried out explosives tests. The concrete walls are 3.5m (11.5ft) thick. The site is open to visitors. (Heimdal).

6. The four casemates at the Azeville battery (2./HKAR 1261), commanded by Leutnant Kattnig, were equipped with French-made 105mm guns. The site has been preserved and is open to visitors (museum). Note the remnants of the imitation stone painted on the casemates. (Heimdal).

Musée de la Liberté, avenue de la Plage, 50310 Quinéville.
Tel. +33 (0)233 214044.
Open daily, March to November from 10.00 to 18.00, June to September from 09.30 to 19.30.

Musée du Débarquement Utah Beach, 50480 Sainte-Marie-du-Mont.
Tel. +33 (0)233 715335.
Open June to September, all day from 09.30 to 19.30.
April, May and June from 10.00 to 12.30 and from 14.00 to 18.00.
From November 15 to March 31, weekends, public holidays and school vacations only, from 10.00 to 12.30 and from 14.00 to 17.30.

1. American paratrooper running towards the church at Sainte-Mère-Église, covered by one of his comrades. (NA/Heimdal).

2. Badge of 82nd Airborne Division.

3. American paratroop's metal insignia.

82nd Airborne Division

This airborne division landed with plenty of experience behind it. It was originally an infantry division and as such had taken part in the Great War. Its name "All American" refers to the fact that the men were drawn from all the states of the Union. After being reformed in May 1942, on August 16, 1942 the personnel of 82nd Infantry Division was split in two to form two airborne divisions: 82nd "All American" Airborne Division and 101st "Screaming Eagles" Airborne Division. The 82nd was sent to Morocco on May 10, 1943 for action in Tunisia. It was later dropped over Sicily on July 10, 1943 and over Italy, near Salerno, on September 13, 1943. The division arrived in Liverpool on April 22, 1944 to play its part in Operation Overlord.

On June 6, 1944, the divisional commander was Major General Matthew Ridgway, in charge of three parachute infantry regiments (505th, 507th and 508th PIR), one airlanding regiment (325th Glider Infantry Regiment), artillery (319th Glider Artillery Battalion to support 508th PIR, 320th Artillery Battalion to support 507th PIR, and 456th Parachute Artillery Battalion to support 505th PIR).

While 101st Airborne Division was dropped to the west of the Utah Beach landing sector to open up the beach exits for 4th Infantry Division, 82nd Airborne Division came down further inland and northwest of 101st Airborne.

This division had a number of assignments:

- to capture and hold Sainte-Mère-Église, an important crossroads on Highway 13; this was the mission of 505th PIR (2,208 men) which further had to mark out LZ W (at Les Forges) for the incoming gliders, also capture and hold two bridges over the Merderet (at La Fière and Chef-du-Pont);

- 507th PIR (1,936 men) was to establish a defensive front to the west of the Merderet and assist 505th PIR in defending the bridges;

- 508th PIR (2,183 men) was to capture and demolish the bridges at Beuzeville, prepare to advance towards the Douve River, and make up a reserve battalion.

A hectic night at Sainte-Mère-Église

Elements of IR 1058 were based in this small Cotentin town. The population was in a state of expectation following regular bombing raids along the coast over the previous few days. On this June 5, 1944, at around eleven pm, the clear night - the moon was full - was lit up by a fire (we shall never know what caused it) at the house of Julia Pommier ("3" on the plan).The alarm bell was ringing as the people formed a chain to put out the fire. A first aircraft formation then flew over the town, followed by another, flying lower. By this time it

4. Dummy paratrooper hanging from the church bell tower in honor of John Steele. (Heimdal photo).

5. The main street at Sainte-Mère-Église (looking northwards, the church is on the right), in June 1944; the place has remained completely unchanged. (Photo, B.Piper/Heimdal).

6. The church at Saint-Mère-Église with the pump used during the night of June 5-6, 1944 to fight the fire at Julie Pommier's house. (Heimdal photo).

7. Center of Sainte-Mère-Église, on the night of June 5-6, 1944. René Jamard and Jules Lemenicier were killed during the battle. (Heimdal plan).

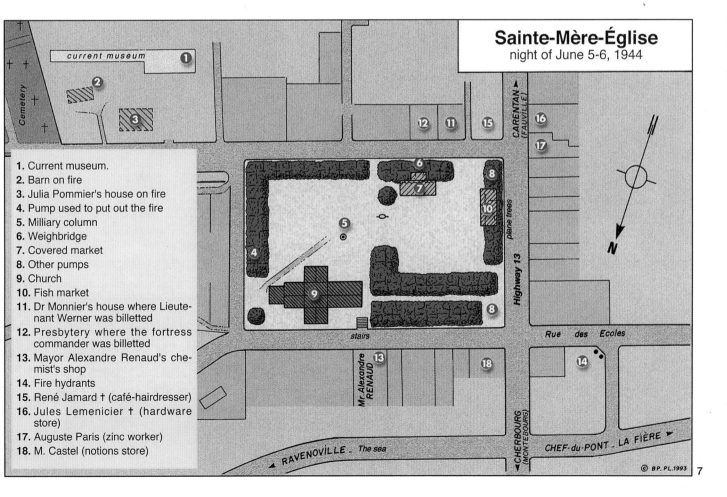

Sainte-Mère-Église
night of June 5-6, 1944

1. Current museum.
2. Barn on fire
3. Julia Pommier's house on fire
4. Pump used to put out the fire
5. Milliary column
6. Weighbridge
7. Covered market
8. Other pumps
9. Church
10. Fish market
11. Dr Monnier's house where Lieutenant Werner was billetted
12. Presbytery where the fortress commander was billetted
13. Mayor Alexandre Renaud's chemist's shop
14. Fire hydrants
15. René Jamard † (café-hairdresser)
16. Jules Lemenicier † (hardware store)
17. Auguste Paris (zinc worker)
18. M. Castel (notions store)

© BP.PL.1993

1. Afternoon of June 7. These paratroopers coming from the south pass through Sainte-Mère-Église on horses they have picked up on the way. (NA/Heimdal).

2. Lieutenant Colonel Vandervoort, CO of 505th P.I.R.'s 2nd Battalion, walking with a crutch, having injured his left ankle. (NA/Heimdal).

3. Major General M.B. Ridgway. (US Army).

was one in the morning and the fire had spread to the wooden barn next door. Suddenly, coming from the west, a throbbing noise gradually became louder, covering the bell, and then very low-flying aircraft appeared: it was the third wave; corollas of different colors loomed in the sky lit up by the

Major-General Matthew B. Ridgway

He was born at Fort Monroe, Virginia on March 3, 1895 and finished at the US Military Academy in April 1917. He held several commands overseas, in China, in the Philippines and in Nicaragua. Upon graduating from Staff College, he was appointed to the general staff, where he remained until January 1942. On June 26, 1942, he was given command of 82nd Infantry Division which became an airborne division. He commanded the division in action in north Africa, Sicily and Italy. For Overlord, he preferred to join the airdrop with his men rather than come in by glider. He landed in a field west of Sainte-Mère-Église. In August 1944, he was put in command of XVIII Airborne Corps which he led into battle in the Ardennes, during the Rhine crossing, in the Ruhr pocket and on the Elbe until the Americans linked up with the Soviets on May 2, 1945. After the war, he became commander-in-chief in the Mediterranean. He commanded US Eighth Army in Korea in 1950 and became commander-in-chief in Korea on April 11, 1951. In May 1952, he succeeded Dwight D. Eisenhower as commander-in-chief of the Allied Forces in Europe. He was made US Army chief-of-staff on August 15, 1953 and retired on June 30, 1955 at the end of a brilliant career. He died on July 26, 1993 at the age of 98.

4. During the afternoon of June 6, 1944, Major Crandell set up a field hospital at Château de Colombières, southeast of Sainte-Mère-Église; this color photo was taken at the time. (Heimdal coll.).

5. The museum at Sainte-Mère-Église recalls the American airborne operations. The display includes a Waco glider and a C.47. (Heimdal photo).

flames. "Paratroopers!" It was 00.15 (British time, 01.15 French time). 506th PIR dropped two sticks over the town. It was total chaos as the Germans opened fire on the paratroops. On Mayor Alexandre Renaud's recommendation, the civilians dived for cover. A third stick (of 505th PIR's Company "F") arrived twenty minutes later; Sergeant

Ray was killed on hitting the ground by a burst of machine-gun fire and Pfc Blankenship came down straight into the blazing house. Shearer fell into a tree and was killed instantly, while a dozen bodies were left hanging from the trees. Private John Steele was wounded by shrapnel in the left foot and drifted towards the bell tower, snarling his parachute on it. At the time, Rudolf May, a German soldier, was in the bell tower but did not fire at John Steele for fear of being spotted, for he had seen down below his buddy Alfons Jakl killed by an American paratrooper as he landed. John Steele was in fact captured by the Germans but escaped a few days later. Finally, the German soldiers mustered in three ranks on the square and left the village uncertain as to what was going on, withdrawing to Château de Fauville (a kilometer to the south). Soon, American paratroops, particularly I Company of 505th PIR, joined up to the east of the village before entering it. The village was invested by 505th PIR's 3rd Battalion (3/505) which landed at DZ O to the west at 02.03. An hour later, Lieutenant-Colonel Krause had gathered 158 men with whom he set about capturing Sainte-Mère-Église, a mission accomplished at five. The men of this regiment's 2nd Battalion (2/505) landed on Norman soil at the earlier time of 00.51. Their CO, Lieutenant-Colonel Vandervoort, sustained an injury to the left ankle. His men carried him off, leaning on his rifle, in a folding munitions trailer. His battalion was to provide protection for Sainte-Mère-Église 2km (1mi) to the north, by establishing itself at Neuville-au-Plain. Vandervoort moved on to Sainte-Mère-Église at 10.00, by which time the Germans had already launched their counter-attacks. The village was the scene of a fierce battle, with a number of civilian casualties. The German attacks, none of

them successful, continued until late afternoon. The little village of Sainte-Mère-Église had just found a place in the history books.

La Fière and the Merderet River

Further west, the way forward was blocked by the inundated Merderet valley. There were several bridges across it, including one at La Fière. Northwest of this valley, 507th PIR carried out the most disastrous airdrop that night at around 02.30, when many paratroopers were scattered and landed in the marshes, with most of their equipment lost as well. However, while 1/505's objective was the **La Fière bridge**, some of 507th PIR assembled north of La Fière in support of 1/505. As for 508th PIR, the men were scattered all over the area and only Lieutenant-Colonel Shanley was able to capture a strongpoint, near Hill 30. The capture of the La Fière bridge was the task of 505th PIR's A Company, which was to link up with the forces of 507th PIR on the west bank. This objective was achieved at 06.00, and the assault was launched an hour later. General Gavin arrived with reinforcements at about 08.30. The bridge and causeway were captured and secured two hours later. Towards noon, came a German counter-attack from the west bank with two Panzer-Abteilung 100 tanks. Both tanks were knocked out. The bridge was victoriously held, and became the key to further progress westward to Pont-l'Abbé, Saint-Sauveur-le-Vicomte and Barneville.

6. At Saint-Marcouf, north-east of Sainte-Mère-Église, an officer of 101st Airborne listens to information from a civilian. The Americans were often mistrustful, having been warned to watch out for "collaborators". (DAVA/Heimdal).

507 505 502
La Fière
508 Ste Mère-Église
506
Hiéville
Vierville
501

Carentan

The American Sector after D-Day

An HM2 105mm self-propelled howitzer opens fire. Nicknamed the "Priest", these guns mounted on a tank chassis were excellent rapid intervention weapons. (DAVA/Heimdal).

From June 7 to 9

In the Omaha Beach sector, on **June 7**, the fighting was still going on near the coast at Colleville-sur-Mer. Further south, Formigny on Highway 13 had been reached. At Vierville, troops of 2nd Infantry Division landed in turn. On **June 8**, the linkup was finally made with the Rangers at the Pointe du Hoc where mopping-up operations were completed by noon. The port of Grandcamp was captured. The men in this sector linked up with British troops on **June 9**. That same day at 05.00, elements of 29th Division entered Isigny.

In the Utah Beach sector, the assault forces linked up with the paratroops at Sainte-Mère-Église towards noon on **June 7**. The GIs seized the Azeville battery and reached Montebourg on **June 9**. To the west, the paratroops of 82nd Airborne, who had been pinned down at La Fière, crossed the Merderet River that same day.

From June 10 to 30

The paratroops of 101st Airborne finally entered Carentan, a town defended by German 6th Parachute Regiment, on **June 12**. The two American beachheads had now joined up. VII Corps could now ad-

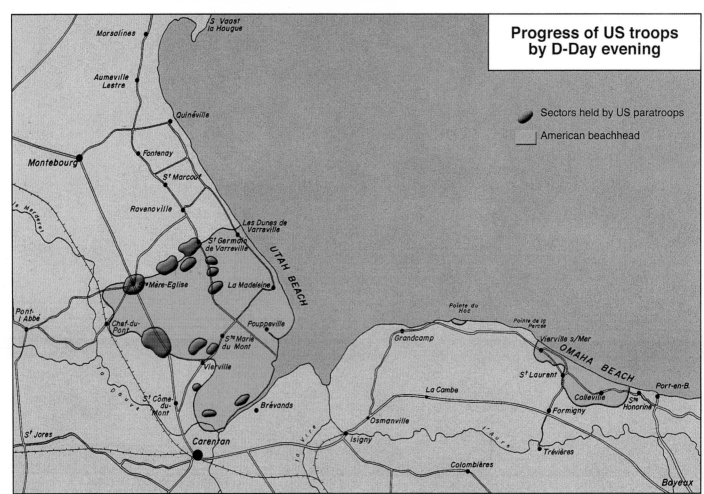

Progress of US troops by D-Day evening

⬤ Sectors held by US paratroops

▢ American beachhead